Decorating

YOUR FIRST HOME

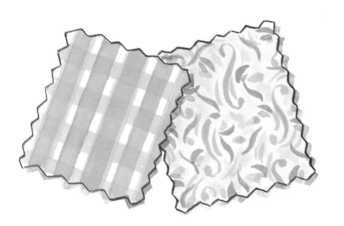

STYLE ON A BUDGET

Decorating

YOUR FIRST HOME

CAROLINE ATKINS

CASSELL

A CASSELL BOOK

Cassell
Wellington House
125 Strand
London WC2R OBB

Designed by Maggie Aldred
Illustrations by Val Hill

Distributed in the United States
by Sterling Publishing Co., Inc.
387 Park Avenue South, New York, New York 10016–8810

Distributed in Australia
by Capricorn Link (Australia) Pty Ltd
2/13 Carrington Road
Castle Hill
NSW 2154

British Library Cataloguing-in-Publication Data
A catalogue record for this book is available from the British Library

ISBN 0-304-34746-9

Typeset by MS Filmsetting Limited

Printed and bound in Slovenia

Acknowledgments
The publishers would like to thank the following for their help in
providing colour photographs:
BhS (p. 31); Cologne & Cotton (p. 105); Crown Paints (pp. 21, 45, 61,
87, 110); Crucial Trading (p. 35); Dorma (pp. 24, 121); Dulux
(pp. 18–19, 65, 66–7, 100–1, 116); Elizabeth Whiting Associates (pp. 9, 37, 57,
62, 72–3, 82–3, 75, 80, 97, 107); Fired Earth (pp. 40–1); GP & J Baker
Ltd (p. 2); Mazda Lighting (pp. 27, 29); Sanderson (pp. 50, 88, 93, 113,
115); Swish (p. 53).
Front cover Crown Paints, GP & J Baker, Swish
Back cover Dulux

Contents

─────

Introduction

It's all yours – so where do you begin? It may be exciting to have the keys to your own home, and know it's yours to decorate as you want, but it's also a daunting prospect if you've never done it before. You'll probably have a mind full of jumbled likes and dislikes, ideas snatched from other people's homes and pictures in magazines, prejudices against the furnishings you grew up with or had to put up with in rented accommodation. You're torn between wanting to do things your own way and needing the advice of others who've already tried their hand at decorating. You want to try something different, but with a reasonably secure guarantee that it's going to work. Above all, you want to enjoy it – and you can. This is where the fun starts. *Decorating Your First Home* is not a book to read all at once: you should work through it in the same way as you'll look at the house itself, first considering the overall shape and the features that give it its character, then focusing on individual rooms and specific details. You'll want to dip into different chapters as you plan each area, and you'll need to refer back to the general information sections to remind yourself of the key planning points and likely trouble spots. There are pictures of finished rooms to inspire you at each step of the way.

First Things First

There's no magic formula for decorating a home. There are no foolproof instructions that can beat your own instinctive knowledge that you've got what you want and that it suits you. What you do need is confidence, and the aim of this book is to give you that confidence, with guidelines to help you discover your own taste as you make the basic decisions involved. Working your way through it, you'll be able to build up a clear picture of your likes and dislikes in colours, fabrics, patterns and furniture design, and gradually put together a style of your own.

A first home isn't quite like any other – it has all the excitement of a new beginning, and you can't wait to put your own stamp on it. And the big advantage you've got over more experienced decorators is that you haven't already amassed too many possessions and furnishings to limit your options.

GETTING TO KNOW YOUR HOME
Establishing your own style means starting at the beginning – with the house itself. Before you can make any decorative plans for it, you need to form a clear idea of the character of the place, its layout, the existing decoration and furnishings.

Is the building old or new? Are the rooms four-square and practical, or crooked and cottagey? How high are the ceilings? How big are the windows? Are there any built-in features like fireplaces and picture rails to be taken into account?

Try to look at the house completely objectively. It may be difficult if it's already painted in a colour you can't bear, or fitted with a carpet you know you can't afford to replace, but don't be put off: at this stage you mustn't let yourself feel limited. The only things that are more or less fixed are the size and shape of the house. Your furniture, your colour schemes, your curtains and pictures and ornaments are going to make it your own.

When you have a clear 'map' of the place outlined in your mind, you can start filling it in with the elements you already know about. That carpet you can't afford to replace, for instance – if you're happy to keep it, bear in mind that your other furnishings will have to match it. (Even if you're not happy to keep it, make sure that you check the condition of the floor underneath before you tear it up!) Have you a favourite picture you want to hang in the sitting room? A set of china you'd like to display? Even a cast-off sofa inherited from relations? All these will have to fit into your plan like the pieces of a jigsaw.

▶ *Style and practicality will have to work together every step of the way when you're decorating your first home. You'll have to choose colours, furniture, flooring and accessories to suit each individual room and make the most of the way you're going to use it.*

PLANNING HOW YOU'LL USE IT

Practical and lifestyle considerations need to be taken into account too. Which rooms will be for relaxing and entertaining? Do you want a spare bedroom, or would the extra space be better employed as a study or separate dining room? Which areas are earmarked as workspace? In a small home, work and play areas may have to overlap, a single room doing double duty for both. If you've a bit more space to play around with, you can afford to be bolder with your decorating plans.

As your 'map' takes shape, it's building up a framework within which you can start to experiment with your decorating ideas. Keep a running list of all the basics you're going to have to buy: table and chairs, a sofa, beds and bedding, carpets if necessary (remember that, even if you prefer stripped floors, flat leases or residents' regulations often insist on carpeting to reduce noise levels). Is there enough built-in storage to cope with clothes, linens and cleaning equipment, or are you going to need extra cupboards and shelves of your own? As well as starting to think about suitable styles, you'll find it useful to begin planning your budget as early as possible, taking account of unavoidable expenses so that you have a clearer picture of where you can cut corners and costs.

Remember that there's no hurry to get started. The longer you give yourself to get a feel for the house, the easier you'll find it to make decisions that will work both practically and decoratively – and the less likely you'll be to make expensive mistakes.

The only real factors likely to influence the speed you want to work at are practical ones. You'll need a working kitchen and bathroom from the beginning, for instance. They may not be quite the way you envisaged them, but as long as they're serviceable you can leave the decorative decisions until you're more sure of what you want. And of course if there is any structural work to be done, this should be got out of the way before there is any decoration for it to interfere with. There's no point in painting and wallpapering a room and then having to dismantle your handiwork to make way for a damp-proof course.

GETTING TO KNOW WHAT YOU LIKE

When it comes to decorative decisions, what matters is that you like the result, so the most important thing is to get to know your own taste.

This book helps by suggesting styles for each room, with advice on how to put together a similar look in your own home, but to make the most of it you also want to start assembling your own style, finding your own pointers and references from among everyday objects and possessions.

It takes a while, but you'll gradually find yourself trusting your judgment more confidently – and there's plenty of room for the individual view. There was a time when you hadn't really any choice: tables had four legs, chairs came with arms or without, and you painted your house whatever colour everyone else was painting theirs. It was easier in some ways, but ultimately much less satisfying, and it didn't allow for any variation in the style of the building – or in your budget. Now that furnishing has broken free of the rules, you have to make the decisions for yourself, but that means you can devise a scheme tailored exactly to suit your home.

COLLECTING YOUR THOUGHTS

Start by compiling a scrapbook of ideas that appeal to you – a loose-leaf file is best, so that you can slot in extra suggestions as you come across them. Collect pictures from magazines, fabric and wallpaper samples, paint colours (paint patches of colour on to paper so that you get a

---

▶ *You'll gradually become more confident about choosing colours and patterns. Fabric shops and wallpaper books are full of inspiring ideas, and you can experiment with sample patches of paint on scrap paper to help you find colours that match.*

▲ *Start a scrapbook of ideas in a loose-leaf binder so that you can add to them easily and make notes. Individual pages can be removed to take shopping when you want to match colours and patterns.*

more realistic idea of how they'll look *in situ*), postcards and photos. The most unexpected places become sources of inspiration: a holiday snap of Mediterranean skies and bright potted geraniums, sheets of patterned gift wrap chosen for a birthday present, a street of houses all painted different colours, even a random-coloured row of books on a shelf.

Then of course there are other people's houses. Make a mental note of features you like, watch for colours and fabrics that work together, try to establish the various elements that are at play when you find a room particularly comfortable or attractive – and then think realistically about whether the same kind of look would work in your home.

To begin with, you'll find yourself chasing all sorts of ideas, often diverse and sometimes conflicting. You may admire a plain white room with minimal furnishings one day, and the next day hanker after a traditional setting complete with old-fashioned knick-knacks and lace curtains. Don't worry: even the most experienced designer can be subject to changes of mind. Your final decision will be a combination of what you want, what you need and what you can afford – and as long as you give yourself time and keep the overall shape of the room in mind, everything will eventually fall into place.

The ultimate test of confidence will be when you feel able to combine selective elements from different styles, but for the moment just collect your ideas together and see what they suggest to you.

As your scrapbook fills up you'll see patterns emerging. Even if the pictures and samples you collect seem to have very little in common at the time, there will be similarities and recurring themes – a preference for abstract patterns or natural textures, for modern-style window

PLANNING CHECKPOINTS
● Assess the basic character and style of the building.

● Think about your lifestyle and establish how you'll want to use different areas of the space.

● Start collecting a scrapbook of ideas and pictures you like – anything from fabric fragments to holiday postcards.

● Decide what features of the place you want – or are prepared – to keep as they are.

● Make a list of problem areas and plan a budget to deal with them.

● Decide what you can tackle yourself and what needs professional help.

● Plan a room-by-room running order. In houses it's best to work from the top downwards so that you can clear up the rubble as you go. In a flat or apartment you can decide which rooms you want finished first according to how quickly you're going to need them.

● Take your time: don't make rushed decisions. You may find that your idea of what you want changes as you get used to living in your new home.

dressing or old-fashioned furniture – and most noticeably for particular colour combinations. You're starting to develop your own style, and colour will be one of its most distinctive signposts.

PRACTICAL DECORATING

When you start planning how to decorate a room, you are probably thinking mainly of the walls. These are what gives the room its overall effect, by providing a background colour. The chapters on individual rooms and on colour and pattern offer advice on the best options for specific areas, but you'll have a basic choice to make between paint and wallpaper.

Painting is cheaper, quicker, easier and gives you a more versatile range of colours – all you have to do is make sure that you pick the right type for the job. Paper has the advantage of adding pattern if you want it, and gives a better-looking finish to a less-than-perfect wall surface.

Paintwork

All the various paints available, whatever their trade names, fall into two main categories: gloss and emulsion. Gloss paints are oil-based, soluble with white spirit and give a washable surface. Emulsion paints are water-soluble.

Liquid gloss Used mainly for wood and metal, and gives a very shiny finish. Needs an undercoat, and bare wood must be primed first (if possible, use a combined primer and undercoat as this will save you drying time). Coverage per

▲ *Paint manufacturers' colour cards are invaluable when you're putting colours together and deciding on the exact shade you want. These can go in your ideas book too. Buy sample pots of colours you like and try them out in larger patches to get a better impression – remember they may dry to a slightly different shade.*

litre: 17 square metres (183 square feet).

Non-drip gloss Mainly for wood and metal, and also useful for plastic surfaces such as guttering and drainpipes. Gives a high-shine finish, and has a gelatinous texture that will not drip or run when you're applying it. Doesn't need an undercoat, but bare wood must be primed first. Coverage per litre: 12–15 square metres (130–162 square feet).

Self-undercoating gloss Used for wood, metal and plastic. Gives a high-shine finish and covers most colours with a single coat. Coverage per litre: 10 square metres (108 square feet).

Eggshell Oil-based paint that gives a less shiny finish than gloss. Washable, but not as easy to

▲ *Collect postcards and pictures from magazines that give you ideas for colours and styles.*

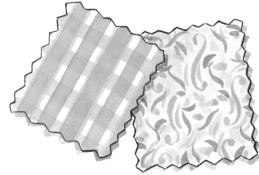

▲ *Most shops will give free samples of fabric and wallpaper for you to take home and try out in situ. If it's patterned, make sure that you ask for a large enough sample to get a clear idea of the whole design.*

clean as gloss. Can be used on walls or as a more subtle alternative to gloss for woodwork and metal. Doesn't need an undercoat, but you'll probably need at least two coats for good coverage, and bare wood must be primed first. Coverage per litre: 16 square metres (172 square feet).

Vinyl silk emulsion Suitable for walls and ceilings. Gives a silky, low-sheen finish that is good for damp, steamy walls in bathrooms and kitchens as it can be wiped clean. The silky finish emphasizes the wall surface, so it's not so good where you want to disguise flaws, but excellent for highlighting the design of a relief-patterned paper. Doesn't need an undercoat. Coverage per litre: 13–14 square metres (140–150 square feet).

PROBLEM SOLVING

If you've taken time to get to know what you want, and not made rushed decisions, you should avoid costly mistakes such as buying large amounts of the wrong fabric. But there will still be times when the going gets tough – when you decide you hate the colour you've painted your sitting room, or when you find you need more bathroom tiles than you ordered and the shop tells you the line has been discontinued.

Don't panic when you run into trouble: most problems can be put right with just a little extra work, and some of them may actually end up better than the idea you started with. The secret is to be flexible and think laterally. The chapter on Colour and Pattern has ideas for putting colour-scheming mistakes right, and the chapter on Last Details is full of accessories and finishing touches that will make a co-ordinated scheme out of a room that's lost its way.

Vinyl matt emulsion The most common choice for walls and ceilings. Has a soft, matt finish that helps disguise uneven surfaces. Doesn't need an undercoat. Coverage per litre: 14–15 square metres (150–162 square feet).

Specialist kitchen and bathroom paint Basically an emulsion paint, but with a high acrylic content that makes it more washable and a mild fungicide to prevent mould growth. Gives a silky but low-sheen finish. Coverage per litre: 16 square metres (172 square feet).

The most practical working order to follow for paintwork is: ceiling first; followed by walls; then doors and windows; radiators; and finally skirting or base boards and any other decorative woodwork. Start painting the room in a corner nearest the window, and work away from the light. Using a roller is the easiest way to get an even surface when you're covering large areas like walls and ceilings, but you'll need brushes for smaller areas and woodwork. Use the right size brush for the area you're tackling: a narrow 12-mm ($\frac{1}{2}$-in) brush for window frames and detailing; a 100-mm (4-in) brush for larger wood areas such as doors and panelling; and a 50-mm (2-in) brush for most other jobs.

Wallpaper
Many wallpapers are not paper at all but vinyl or PVC, so check the pasting and hanging instructions on the individual roll label, as these will vary. Some wallcoverings come pre-pasted and the cut lengths can simply be immersed in a trough of water before hanging. Embossed or textured papers, such as Anaglypta, have come back into fashion in recent years and are a good way of adding a little more interest to a plain-coloured wall.

The measuring-up table opposite will help you calculate how many rolls you need. Remember that for larger patterns you will need more rolls to allow for matching up the design – ask for advice in the shop before you buy.

Always start next to a window and work away from the source of light, in both directions, finishing in the darkest corner. If you're using a patterned paper in a room with a chimney breast, start this wall by centring a length on the chimney breast and then work outwards into the alcoves.

Never try to hang a full width of paper around a corner – always hang it in two parts. Let each of the two pieces overlap slightly on to the next wall, and then trim off the excess down the corner line to give a neat finish.

Panelling

If the wall surface is a real problem, wood panelling is another option you should consider. This is a brilliant way of covering up bad plastering or an uneven finish. Panelling can be bought at DIY centres along with complete fitting instructions. Tongue-and-groove planking and old-fashioned-style rectangular panels are both available in sections that slot together to provide a panelled area as large as you want. Fixing wood like this up to dado-rail level will neaten the lower half of the walls, and it can then be painted to match the upper part.

▲ *Wood panelling is a foolproof way of covering up a damaged or badly plastered wall surface. It needs to be fixed to wood battens running at right-angles to the panels. Wood moulding can then be added as a trim to hide the fixing points.*

MEASURING UP Use this table to work out how many rolls of wallpaper you will need. (Figures based on a standard roll of around 10.05 m/11 yd long and 530 mm/2 ft 1 in wide.)

WALLS (height from skirting)	The complete distance around the room **including the doors and windows**																		
	9 30	10 34	12 38	13 42	14 46	15 50	16 54	17 58	18 62	19 66	21 70	22 74	23 78	24 82	26 86	27 90	28 94	30 98	**(metres)** **(feet)**
2.15–2.3 m 7 ft–7 ft 6 in	4	5	5	6	6	7	7	8	8	9	9	10	10	11	12	12	13	13	**rolls**
2.3–2.45 m 7 ft 6 in–8 ft	5	5	6	6	7	7	8	8	9	9	10	10	11	11	12	13	13	14	
2.45–2.6 m 8 ft–8 ft 6 in	5	5	6	7	7	8	9	9	10	10	11	12	12	13	14	14	15	15	
2.6–2.75 m 8 ft 6 in–9 ft	5	5	6	7	7	8	9	9	10	10	11	12	12	13	14	14	15	15	
2.75–2.9 m 9 ft–9 ft 6 in	6	6	7	7	8	9	9	10	10	11	12	12	13	14	14	15	15	16	
2.9–3.05 m 9 ft 6 in–10 ft	6	6	7	8	8	9	10	10	11	12	12	13	14	14	15	16	16	17	
3.05–3.2 m 10 ft–10 ft 6 in	6	7	8	8	9	10	10	11	12	13	13	14	15	16	16	17	18	19	
CEILINGS	To calculate the number of rolls required, work out the area in square metres and divide by five.																		

Colour and Pattern

The colours you put into your home will bring it to life like a painting book. Imagine each room as a series of blank outlines: walls, windows, furniture, woodwork. Now try filling in patches of colour – even plain black and white – and you'll see each item individually defined.

Colour is the most versatile tool at the decorator's disposal. You can change it, adapt it, move it from one place to another and use it in any quantity you want. Putting colours together is great fun, so don't be intimidated by terms like 'colour theory' and 'the science of colour'. This chapter outlines the only rules you need – showing the effect various colours can have when used in different settings, and explaining why certain colour pairings work better than others.

MAGIC DECORATING COLOURS
Some colours make an instant impression on a room. They can make a room seem larger or smaller, colder or warmer, and they can make the occupants feel anything from stimulated to relaxed to downright depressed! So as well as choosing colours for themselves, you need to consider the effect they will have.

Visual Tricks
Furnishing colours can be divided into 'advancing' and 'receding' shades. In general, dark shades are advancing and lighter colours will have a receding effect. 'Advancing' shades appear to make a surface nearer than it actually is, so if you use these on walls and ceilings, the room will seem smaller. 'Receding' shades have the opposite effect, making walls and ceilings look further away and therefore giving a more spacious feel.

The impression will also be influenced by whether the shades are 'warm' or 'cool'. The colour spectrum – red, orange, yellow, green, blue, indigo, violet – is 'warm' at the red end and 'cool' at the blue end. Green is the crossover point in the middle, with yellowy greens feeling quite warm, and bluey greens being much cooler. Violet makes another crossover point. If you imagine the spectrum as a complete circle, you end up with what designers and artists call the 'colour wheel', and you'll see that violet will start to become warmer again as it merges back into red.

The most obvious feature of the way these colours work is that they literally make a room feel warmer or cooler, so warm colours can create a welcoming, cosy impression and cool colours will be more restful and refreshing. But a secondary effect is that warm colours are advancing and cool colours are receding.

So the most advancing colours are dark colours from the warm end of the spectrum and the most receding colours are light shades from the cool end. Painting the walls dark red is the quickest way to make a room look smaller, and painting them white with a hint of blue will make it seem instantly larger. This is obviously an extreme example, but the basic principle is the key to choosing decorating colours for different rooms. Once you understand it, you'll be able to use colour to create all sorts of effects.

Suiting the Colour to the Room
Think about the structure and shape of the room itself and what you plan to use it for, and then

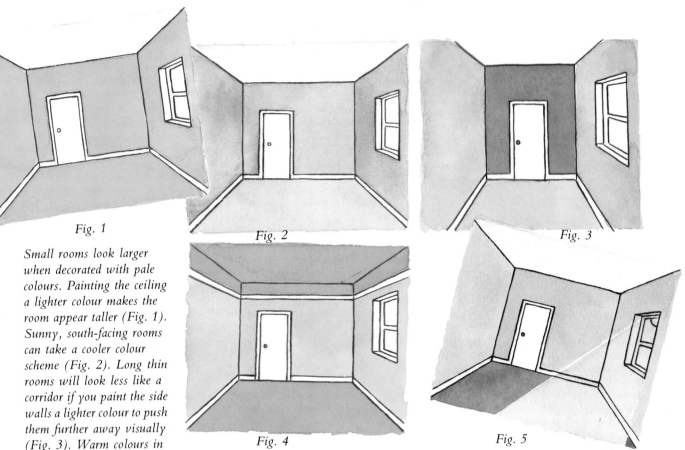

Fig. 1

Fig. 2

Fig. 3

Fig. 4

Fig. 5

Small rooms look larger when decorated with pale colours. Painting the ceiling a lighter colour makes the room appear taller (Fig. 1). Sunny, south-facing rooms can take a cooler colour scheme (Fig. 2). Long thin rooms will look less like a corridor if you paint the side walls a lighter colour to push them further away visually (Fig. 3). Warm colours in darker shades will make a room cosier, especially if you paint the ceiling in a dark colour (Fig. 4). A north-facing room that doesn't get much sun will benefit from warm colours in light, bright tones (Fig. 5).

consider the colours that will suit it.

Which way does it face, and how big are the windows? A north-facing or small-windowed room may feel dark and cold. Decorating a room like this in a light colour will instantly help, and a colour from the warmer end of the spectrum – such as a pale pink or yellow – will also take the edge off the chill. At the other extreme, a south-facing room with large windows may feel too bright for comfort, in which case you can add a hint of blue to cool it down.

Is the room going to be a work area or a place to relax and unwind? Are you trying to create an informal, welcoming atmosphere or somewhere smart and elegant? One of the most interesting things about colour is the way different colour groups can induce different psychological moods. Because of these effects, certain colours have become associated with particular rooms and effects.

MOOD CHANGERS

Yellows are stimulating and refreshing and will make the coldest or gloomiest room look sunny and cheerful, so they're good for kitchens, work areas and daytime living rooms. If you find the brighter shades too much, try a pale primrose or a sandy ochre to give a softer effect.

Pinks are soft and restful – again, useful in a living-room colour scheme (especially if you want to create a more elegant, less everyday look) and their calming effect also makes them good for bedrooms. To avoid too sugary an effect, a yellowy pink such as peach is a good alternative.

Green was out of favour as a furnishing colour for a long time, but it's a clever way of conjuring up a sense of the garden or countryside

17

(particularly in combination with pink). Use a light, fresh green in a city apartment, and you can give it a much more open, outdoor feel. It's especially good for rooms that lead on to gardens or balconies.

Light blues and greens and most shades of turquoise are generally cool and restful – good for bedrooms and areas for daytime relaxing. Because of their association with water, they also have a natural place in kitchens and bathrooms, where they look refreshing and practical.

Darker blues and greens give a more formal impression. These shades work well in dining rooms and other areas planned for evening use. If your bedroom is going to be strictly a night-time place, you can use a colour like this to create a night-sky effect that's wonderfully dramatic but still very restful.

Reds are the most stimulating colour group of all – definitely not conducive to a good night's sleep! They can be used for a wide range of effects from bright, practical shades for kitchens, to rich terracotta or burgundy, both of which look wonderful in cosy dining rooms and studies.

Neutral Territory

Neutral shades have acquired the reputation of being 'safe' decorating colours, but they're not as easy as they sound, because – apart from white – they're never *completely* neutral. Creams, for instance, vary from pink tones to yellowy green with completely different effects. Although it's basically a light colour, a cream from the greener end of the range can actually appear quite dull, grey and depressing in an area that doesn't get

---

▶ *Soft pastel colours are always restful and easy to live with – and they mix well too. (Think how wonderful all the different shades of ice cream look lined up in a shop window!) There's very little pattern here: floor, walls and furnishings are all plain. But the use of straight lines is very effective, and gives the room a distinctive shape. The rug is striped, the long blinds have a strong vertical line as well as their horizontal slats, and the struts of the director's chairs add diagonal lines as well.*

18

much light. Greys should be avoided in a north-facing room for the same reason. Darker neutrals such as browns and beiges are difficult to use over large areas, but their warm tones can be very effective if they're carefully chosen. See the living room on page 67 for a good example of this.

PUTTING COLOURS TOGETHER

The most important thing about the colours you're going to live with is that you like them. If you're in any doubt about your colour-scheming ability, just remember that you do it every day when you decide what clothes to wear. For some reason furnishing colours have acquired a sense of mystique, but putting colours together in your home is as simple as putting together an outfit.

The secret is not to try to combine too many colours at first. A fabric chosen for a sofa or curtains will provide you with a basic palette from which you can pick up individual shades to use elsewhere in the room.

Collect your ideas for each room together – keeping each set on a separate page of your scrapbook – so that you can build up a complete picture of the scheme and assess how well it works. Staple fabric, wallpaper and border samples on to the page and paint on patches of colours you're considering. If you find just the colour you want in a postcard or a magazine picture, add that to the page too for reference.

A colour theme for a particular room may be suggested by a favourite picture, or collection of china. (See the individual room chapters for pictures of schemes created around personal possessions.) But inspiration for colour combinations can come from all sorts of random observations too.

Look at the way colours work in a garden, for instance. A flower bed doesn't need to be carefully colour-schemed to look effective: all sorts of shades mixed together make a wonderful show. There's no foundation at all for the old adage that 'blue and green should never be seen' – blues and greens actually work extremely well together as a furnishing combination. Trees and plants are another good example. Leaf colours are never perfectly colour co-ordinated, but the different greens give each other depth and contrast. And as they change with the seasons all sorts of complementary reds and golds appear in the mix too.

Certain colours make natural combinations and are easy to mix. You can use pastel shades in several different colours, for instance, because the contrast is very gentle and they are all basically the same tone. Greens and pinks make a classic country-cottage or garden-room combination. Rich yellowy creams look good with green too. Blues and yellows always appear fresh and pretty together. And yellows and greens both mix surprisingly well with mauves: again, this is a natural flower combination – think of bunches of violets, and the yellow and purple heads of pansies.

Accent Colour

Large blocks of contrasting plain colours will have a jarring effect, so the easiest way to introduce extra colours to your basic scheme is by adding accent colour. This is colour used in small quantities to highlight areas of interest and break up the background shade.

Accent colour is often used for woodwork detail. Picture rails, dado rails, skirting boards (base boards) and window frames picked out in a different shade from the walls will outline the shape of the room and prevent the main colour from feeling flat and monotonous.

The best thing about accent colour is that you can also add it in movable details. Cushions,

▶ *Colours, patterns and textures all work together here to unify the quite different elements of the room. It's important not to forget texture: the rough-plastered wall surface, the weave of the wicker chair and the spattered paint effect on the console table all add their own sense of pattern to the bold fabric design. It's a very brave mix of colours, but the basic red and green theme – carried right through to the picture frame and vases – holds it together and is strong enough not to be upset by the introduction of surprising shades like pink and yellow.*

curtains, lamps and pictures should all be chosen with the overall colour scheme in mind, and as your confidence with colour increases you can add more accessories to try out different effects.

Complementary Colours

As explained above, the safest way to choose accent colours is by sticking to a basic palette inspired by a fabric or some other focal point. But for more variety you can also have great fun experimenting with complementary colours.

Every colour has a complementary colour which is in effect its 'opposite'. Complementary pairings are best demonstrated with the primary colours: red, blue and yellow. The complemen-

tary of each of these is the colour that is made if you mix together the *other* two primaries. So green (mixed from blue and yellow) is the complementary colour to red. Orange (red and yellow) complements blue. And violet (red and blue) complements yellow. In each case placing the complementary colour next to its pair appears to intensify it by contrast. Red makes green look more green, and orange makes blue look more blue, and so on.

Complementary contrasts are too harsh to be used in quantity, but they make very effective accent colour. A green cushion, for instance, can be piped in red. And you can see the pairing working in a subtler way if you think of russet-orange terracotta tiles in a predominantly blue and white kitchen.

Colour Matching

On a practical note, once you're sure of what you want, make sure that you keep a paint colour card or sample of fabric with you when you're shopping to match it. Colours are unbelievably difficult to remember accurately and you will need a visual reminder. Mauves and violets, for instance, can be almost blue or distinctly pink.

It's also a good idea to try paint colours out on a fairly large area before you decide on them, as the balance of the colour is often affected by the quantity used. A blue-green may look exactly the shade you want when you see it on a colour card, but once you've got a whole wall of it you may find that it's gone too far in one direction and looks either too blue or too green.

ADDING PATTERN

The easiest way to introduce pattern is to keep the walls and floor plain and add more detail with fabrics and accessories.

If you're not feeling too confident, you can start by adding a small amount of pattern such as a wallpaper border. And if you're really stuck for inspiration, many manufacturers make it easy for you by putting together completely co-ordinated ranges of fabrics, wallpapers, borders, bed linen – even details like lampshades – so that you don't

---

COLOUR-SCHEMING PROBLEM SOLVERS

● If you make a mistake with paint – either by opting for the wrong colour or by applying it badly – remember that you can always cover your tracks by adding another coat over the top.

● To soften the effect of a paint colour that hasn't turned out quite as you expected, try sponging or colourwashing with a secondary colour over the first.

● Even a colour that's exactly what you want can be overpowering in large doses. To lighten a solid block of colour – for instance, a painted wall – use a contrasting shade to accent woodwork and highlight features.

● Most difficult colours can be offset or complemented with well-chosen accessories. Use cushions, rugs, china and pictures to introduce small amounts of accent colour that balance the effect.

have to worry about what goes with what!

However, patterns aren't difficult to work with if you keep them simple. Like colours, different pattern groups create different effects and have become associated with certain decorative styles.

Stripes and checks form a pattern group that is one of the simplest to use. Plain cotton gingham, mattress ticking and candy stripes are good for practical rooms like kitchens and bathrooms. Plaids and tartans can be made to look more formal, especially if you choose rich colours.

Florals are a traditional furnishing pattern. Large motifs like roses and wisteria will give a formal country-house effect, while smaller sprigs are more informal and cottagey. The two can, however, be mixed quite easily – with a collection of cushions in different florals, or a large flower print curtain trimmed with a border in a smaller motif.

Some of the most beautiful fabrics are based on just a couple of colours. One of the most effective is toile de jouy, an intricate design of figures and scenes in a plain colour on a white or cream background. It was originally French, but it has a similar effect to the Chinese willow pattern in its combination of detail and simplicity.

Texture is very important too. Some fabrics, such as tapestry weaves, have a natural texture which emphasizes their pattern. Others can provide texture or pattern in a plain colour. Rough-surfaced natural weaves such as linen and calico are good for this. There are also plain fabrics that have a definite pattern woven into their make-up: these are described as 'self-patterned' and they provide a more structured sense of texture. Lace does the same job in a much more delicate way.

Mixing Patterns

Patterns are easiest to use if you stick to a single group, so that the overall look stays cohesive. But when you're feeling more confident, you can start experimenting with putting different fabrics together. There are two simple routes to take to prevent the result from being a mess! One is to stick to the same pattern but use different colours;

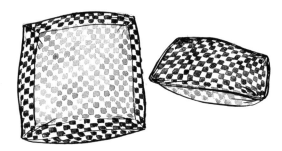

▲ *Cushions are a good way of introducing a small amount of pattern. A simple design such as a check can be livened up by using two different colours – one on each side, for instance, or one for the main fabric and another as a border.*

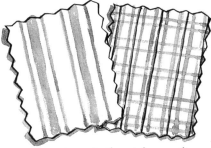

▲ *Different patterns in a similar style – such as stripes and checks, which are both linear – can be combined very effectively.*

▶ *Different florals will work well together, as long as you stick to a basic colour scheme.*

◀ *Stars have appeared on lots of fabrics and wallpapers recently. Try stars and stripes together for a really flamboyant effect!*

23

the other is to combine different patterns in the same basic colours.

Same pattern, different colours This works best with designs that use few colours, such as checks and stripes. Different-coloured ginghams can be combined to make reversible cushion covers – blue and white on one side, perhaps, with green and white on the other. Or you could use a border of blue gingham to trim a yellow curtain.

This is also a very effective way to use toile de jouy. Toile is usually worked in black, blue, green or dark red on white, but the design is so delicate that the overall effect can be almost monochrome. Using two different colours together, such as blue and green, gives more depth and enriches the colour. Again this works well as a curtain trim: try adding a deep pelmet in the contrasting colour. Or use toile in several different colours to make a collection of almost-matching cushions.

Same colour, different patterns Different florals will mix well if you stick to the same colour scheme, but in general it's best if you keep at least one of your patterns quite plain. Checks and stripes work well together as they have the same simple, functional feel. For a more flamboyant effect you can try stars and stripes – it's a mix that's had a highly successful test run!

One of the most innovative and creative pattern combinations in recent years has been florals with checks. It sounds unlikely, but the simplicity of checks creates the perfect balance with a more luxurious flower print. You can see how well the combination works if you look at the curtained-off dining area on page 88.

◀ *Blue and white are classic furnishing colours. These fabrics and wallpapers show the combination in two traditional patterns – florals and checks. Different sizes of check work very effectively together, and you can also combine flowers and checks successfully if you stick to a basic colour scheme like this. In the curtain fabric the check design has been taken a step further, incorporating a flower motif inside each large square.*

COLOUR-SCHEMING CHECKPOINTS

● Take a look at your possessions and make a note of the colours and combinations you like: favourite outfits, a piece of china, book jackets, postcards and pictures.

● Look out for colour combinations that work together naturally – flowers and fruits are a good starting point.

● Try out paint colours on a consistent background to get an idea of how they'll look *in situ* and see if they change as they dry.

● Paint sample patches over a large enough area to get a good impression of the colour – a whole wall of it may look quite different from a small sample on a colour card.

● Make a scrapbook collection of paint samples, fabrics and wallpapers for each room. Mix and match until you find a combination you're happy with.

● Take samples with you when you go shopping to match a colour – it's very difficult to memorize them accurately.

● Take samples of fabric or wallpaper away from shops so that you can check them in the natural light of your own home.

● Learn to trust your own eyes. However convinced you are in principle that you want or don't want a certain shade, or that two particular colours won't work together, if you like what you see then you've got it right.

Lighting

Light gives accent to the colours and shapes of your home – softening outlines or defining angles, altering perspective and completely changing the character of the room according to how it's used.

Lighting, like colour, has a sense of mystique about it. We know what we like when we see it *in situ*, but it can be difficult to work out how to create the same effect in our own homes. If you're looking in despair at a room fitted with a central ceiling pendant and an on/off switch, the ideas in this chapter will provide inspiration for alternative light sources and help you create the scheme you want.

A word of warning: don't leave your lighting decisions until after your decoration work is completed and it's too late to install new wiring. Make them part of your basic room planning so that you can get any necessary electrical work done before you paint or wallpaper. If you're not going to be able to rewire completely, at least make sure that you have plenty of power points in each room, so that you can make full use of all the freestanding lights available.

HOW LIGHT WORKS

Anyone lucky enough to have large, south-facing windows knows the value of good light. As well as giving the occupants a general sense of well-being, it brings out the quality of the room's colours, and highlights the interest and detail of the room's structure.

The quality of natural daylight is very different from that of the artificial lighting we use in our homes (see 'Light Colour and Quality' on page 33), but we can learn a lot from the way it works. Because sunlight reaches different parts of the room at different angles, it casts natural shadows and creates areas of contrast. It's this variety of mood that brings the room to life. However, the added benefit of artificial light is that you can control and vary it to create exactly the level and direction you want.

PLANNING YOUR LIGHTING SCHEME

We need a basic level of light to see our way around. We also need to illuminate specific areas more clearly – to work, read, prepare food, put on make-up. We want to make the room look its best, highlighting good features and disguising less attractive ones. And we want to be able to adapt our lighting to match our mood, providing a setting that's stimulating, restful or just generally comfortable.

To fulfil all these requirements, interior lighting falls into three main categories, providing *background*, *local* and *mood* illumination. Different rooms obviously have different priorities, but an effective scheme combines lights from at least two of these groups.

Background Lighting
Background lighting provides a working level of general visibility, more or less imitating weak sunlight. The disadvantage of the central ceiling light is that – unlike sunlight – it tends to bathe

▶ *Six different sources are at work in this sitting room to provide effective background and mood lighting. Recessed ceiling downlighters give overhead light. The wall-mounted uplighters bounce light off the ceiling and highlight the wall colour and the detail of the border around the top. Table lamps fitted with wide shades cast pools of light at seating level and the picture is lit by a wall-mounted bracket. A hidden floorstanding uplighter illuminates the plant from behind and also casts its shadow on to the ceiling. And a concealed spotlight has been used to highlight the table area.*

the whole room evenly, without much variety, so the effect can be rather characterless.

If you're not in a position to rewire the room and get rid of this central light, your most effective option is to choose a fitting that suits the style of the room and then supplement it with local and mood lighting to add character and contrast. Avoid small shades that look swamped and lost hanging in the middle of a room. For alternative solutions, see the overhead lighting options in 'Choosing Light Fittings' on page 29.

If you're planning your lighting from scratch, you could consider sealing off the central fitting and installing downlighters recessed into the ceiling. You'll have to check that the ceiling is deep enough to take the fitting, and the room will have to be rewired, but a group of discreet downlighters provides an effect that is much more genuinely 'background' light than a more obvious fitting can.

Wall lights can either supplement overhead light or replace it altogether. You'll find that wall lights fitted at several points around the room will supply the same level of illumination as a single overhead light, but because the light source is lower, and nearer furniture height, it's more restful for sitting and dining rooms and bedrooms.

Alternatively you can opt for freestanding table and floor lamps: again, several of these will be as efficient as a single overhead light, but the light will be diffused and softened. The real benefit is that you can move them around the room to find the most effective position – and, of course, you can take them with you when you move (a much more cost-effective option than rewiring for wall lights or downlighters).

Local or Task Lighting

As its name suggests, local or task lighting concentrates the beam on to localized areas to provide light for a specific purpose – reading lamps on desks and fluorescent strips fitted beneath kitchen wall cabinets both fall into this category. Fluorescent tubes are strong enough not to need much directing, but most task lights

---

TRICKS OF THE LIGHT

● **To disguise less-than-perfect walls** Use table lamps and floor-standing uplighters to create pools of light rather than flooding the whole room.

● **To accent a restful wall colour or attractive feature** Fit spots or wall washers angled to catch the glow of the colour and highlight the best view.

● **To make a small room feel larger** Use uplighters or wall washers so that the light grazes the wall in patches rather than illuminating the whole thing – that way it will appear less like a solid barrier. Highlighting a multi-surfaced feature such as a plant in a corner will also help to give more sense of depth to the room.

---

will have an opaque fitting or shade of some sort to direct the light exactly where you want it. A jointed or adjustable lamp such as the traditional Anglepoise is the most obvious example, but spotlights fitted to the walls or ceiling will perform the same function, and can be positioned to illuminate a painting or fireplace.

Mood or Accent Lighting

Mood lighting is illumination used as an accessory, a purely decorative effect designed to highlight the room's features and furnishings. In some cases it can be achieved simply by positioning a light where it accents the colour of a wall or the shape of the room, but you can also make the most of the room's existing decorative features – by fixing a wall bracket over a favourite picture, for instance, or placing a table lamp next to a group of photographs. Similarly an alcove of shelves filled with plants or ornaments can be lit from behind for extra effect.

CHOOSING LIGHT FITTINGS

Depending on what the shade is made of, the light will be directed or diffused to give very different effects. Always see what the shade looks like illuminated before you make a decision.

Whatever fittings you decide on, you'll be able to make the most of the effects they can create if you install dimmer switches to control the light levels. Stark overhead light is greatly improved by being softened like this, and it's an instant way of adding atmosphere.

Overhead Lighting

Central ceiling lights Can be a pendant design on a flex, or a globe or dish fitted flush

▲ *A stand-fitted spotlight will direct accent lighting on plants or ornaments. Well-lit plants look particularly effective, as the leaf surfaces respond to the light at different angles, giving plenty of texture.*

against the ceiling. Make sure that you choose a shade that suits the proportions of the room, and think about what it will look like from below. If the shade gives a clear view of the exposed bulb, one of the large, almost spherical bulbs will look more attractive. Otherwise you're better off with a globe design, or a bowl that reflects the beam outwards and upwards. See also 'Rise-and-fall lights' on page 30.

WHAT SORT OF BULB?

Tungsten filament The traditional all-purpose bulb, available in a range of shapes from the familiar mushroom to an imitation candle flame. It can be used in all standard domestic fittings. The light it emits is produced by the heat of the filament, so the higher the wattage, the brighter and whiter the light.

Tungsten halogen In this bulb the light from the tungsten filament interacts with halogen gas, regenerating the filament and preventing evaporated tungsten particles from blackening the glass. This means that the bulbs last longer, and because they operate at a higher temperature they also give a purer, whiter light from a much lower wattage. Halogen bulbs provide excellent background light when fitted in wall or floorstanding uplighters, and can be used in a concentrated beam for highlighting work surfaces and decorative features. Freestanding halogen lights cannot be run off a standard domestic socket without transformers, which are rather cumbersome, so – if you can – you're better off having them wired in.

Fluorescent tube The big advantage of this is its neat, compact design which – combined with the fact that it doesn't emit much heat – makes it very useful for lighting awkward areas of kitchens, bathrooms and cupboards. It's very energy-efficient, using up to five times less electricity to provide the same amount of light as a tungsten filament bulb.

Rise-and-fall lights Adjustable pendant fittings that can be lowered so that the glow is shed in a more specific direction: for example, over a dining table.

Chandeliers Nowadays these range from the traditional crystal-clustered waterfall to rustic or high-tech designs in wrought iron and carved wood. They can be hung from a central pendant fitting and wired for small electric candle bulbs. They make an overhead light more of a centre-piece, and the multiple light sources soften and diffuse the glow they cast.

Recessed downlighters Discreet spots fitted into the ceiling itself to provide background lighting without drawing attention to the source.

Wall washers Spotlights recessed into the ceiling or slotted on to a ceiling track, and angled so that the beam washes against the wall.

Wall Lights

Brackets and sconces Wall-mounted fittings with individual bulbs, often in pairs. Available in a variety of traditional and contemporary designs, either with shades or candle bulbs.

Uplighters Dish fittings set flush against the wall so that the beam is cast upwards and outwards. Excellent for atmospheric background lighting.

Freestanding Lighting

Floorstanding uplighters Tall lamps with a dish fitting on top to direct the beam upwards so that it reflects off the ceiling and back into the room. The big advantage is their portability – you can add instant background light wherever you need it, as well as highlighting and disguising specific features.

Table lamps Provide pools of light that vary the intensity of the background lighting. Can also be used for reading, and to highlight groups of photos or ornaments.

▶ *The shape of a light fitting and the way the bulb is shaded can be used to create all sorts of effects to match different styles of furnishing.*

Ceiling-recessed downlighter.

Wall-fitted uplighter.

Floorstanding uplighter.

Rise-and-fall pendant.

Picture light.

Ceiling-recessed wall washer.

Track-mounted spotlights.

Recessed kitchen strip light.

Table lamp.

These illustrations show the effect of the light cast by different types of fitting.

Adjustable lamps   For example, Anglepoises. Provide good directional light for task purposes – reading, sewing and so on – and for accenting areas of interest.

Other Light Sources
Spotlights   Can be positioned as clusters, slotted on to tracks or fitted to a stand to provide directional light wherever you need it. Discreet fittings that are easy to conceal in a corner or an alcove. Wall spots can be run off a mains power point with a long flex, so these are a useful option if you're not in a position to rewire.
Picture lights   Individual wall brackets fitted above a picture you want to highlight. The solid metal shade casts the beam directly on to the picture from close range.
Candlelight   Invaluable for adding atmosphere. The soft light and sense of movement can't be matched by any artificial light, so make the most of candlesticks and candelabra when you're relaxing or entertaining.

LIGHT COLOUR AND QUALITY

The effect created by a light source depends on the actual quality and colour of the light it emits as much as on its position and direction. Daylight, for instance, is a fairly cool white – that's why items viewed in daylight are assumed to be in their 'natural' state. A traditional tungsten filament bulb emits a warmer, slightly yellow light: try switching on a tungsten lamp during the day and you can instantly see the contrast between the cooler, whiter, natural light and the area illuminated artificially. And at the other end of the lighting spectrum a fluorescent tube can provide a very cold, quite blue light.

The colours in your home can therefore appear very different under different lights. When you are shopping for paint, you'll often find that the colour charts are displayed in specially lit units letting you switch from simulated 'daylight' to different qualities/levels of artificial light to see how the colours change under each. Think of this when you're choosing fabrics and other furnishings as well. You won't

be able to maintain a constant quality of light in your home, so the important thing is to make sure that the colours you decorate with work equally well together whatever light source they're subjected to. Take samples and swatches home with you and try them out at different times of day and under different types of light.

The reason why halogen has become so popular in recent years is that it is far closer to the colour and tone of daylight than either tungsten or fluorescent lights. This means that, as well as creating a restful and natural feeling, it is also easier to combine with the different colours of your furnishings.

LIGHTING CHECKPOINTS
● Make your lighting decisions before you tackle any other decorative work – you don't want to disrupt newly painted walls to access the wiring.

● Assess the level of natural light and make it work for you with glazed doors, mirrors and so on.

● Establish what roles you need your auxiliary lighting to fulfil. Does the room need background, local or mood lighting – or a combination of two or three of these elements?

● Consider which aspects of the room you want to highlight and/or disguise.

● Decide on the strength of light you need each fitting to provide and the direction in which you want the beam to be cast.

● Ask to see light fittings switched on before you buy, so that you can observe the strength and direction of the beam and gauge its effect.

33

Floors

It's easy to dismiss the floor as a purely functional and therefore relatively uninteresting element of your decorating plans. After all, you're only going to walk all over it! But think of the amount of space it covers. The only part of your furnishings that will present a bigger area to the view are the walls. So in terms of the overall effect, the floor has just as important a part to play as the colour you put on your walls.

Laying any sort of new floor will eat a big chunk out of your budget – and won't be something you can easily change your mind about if you're not happy with the result. Ideally, then, you want something that you're not going to tire of, that's versatile enough to cope with any decorative changes you decide to make later and that won't lose its looks with wear.

If your budget is very tight, one option you might want to consider at this stage is renovating the existing floor. See the instructions on page 38 for sanding wood boards and painting floors.

WHAT SORT OF FLOOR?
Answering the following basic questions will help you decide what sort of floor is best for each room:

● **How much wear will the floor get?** A busy living room will have to put up with much more traffic than a rarely used dining room. Hallways will have to withstand outdoor shoes tramping in and out, whereas bedroom floors may have to cope only with slippers and bare feet.

● **How easy will it be to clean?** Kitchens and halls need surfaces that can be wiped clean of spills and muddy footprints.

● **Is the floor likely to get wet?** Bathrooms and utility rooms need water-resistant floors.

● **Will children be using the room?** Soft floors are non-slip, and more comfortable on the knees if they're crawling or falling over – but remember that you'll want something that's easy to clean as well.

● **How much warmth do you want underfoot?** If you tend to walk around barefoot, remember that some of the hard floors, such as ceramic tiles, may be rather chilly.

● **Will the floor be tiring to stand on for long periods?** Kitchens in particular need a floor that is comfortable underfoot while you're cooking.

● **Are you concerned about noise?** Hard floors will be noisier than soft ones, particularly rigid surfaces like ceramic tiles.

● **Are you going to worry about dropping breakable items?** The harder the floor, the less chance your favourite china has of surviving if you drop it.

● **Will you have to pay professional fitting costs?** Most carpets and many tiled and wood floors need to be laid by a professional, so you'll have to build the extra cost into your budget.

SOFT FLOORS
Soft floors can be divided into two main types: carpet and natural matting. Strictly speaking, the latter is sometimes not very soft at all! But it has the same thickness and resilience as carpet, and offers the same useful qualities of sound absorbency and insulation.

Carpet
The advantages of carpet are obvious: it's comfortable, quiet, a good insulator, and it also gives you the widest colour choice – anything from a neutral background to more decided patterns.

Plain carpet is the most versatile choice, increasing the sense of floor space and providing a flexible background for your furnishings. And light to mid colours are the most practical to live with. Although a very pale shade may suffer from grubby marks, in general a light colour won't show fluff and threads as clearly as a dark background – a very useful consideration if you're not going to be in a position to clean every day!

If you don't want a solid stretch of one colour, a flecked mixture will give a subtle alternative and introduce hints of other shades without adding a definite pattern.

Choosing the right carpet quality The number of different fibres, types of pile and methods of construction used for carpets these days can seem quite bewildering. They can be woven, tufted or bonded. They can have short or long pile, which can be cut, looped or twisted. And they can be made from 100 per cent pure

▲ *A natural coir floor is the perfect match for the cream-and-white scheme in this split-level bedroom. It also provides a tough, kickproof wall surface for the side of the platform, where a softer carpet would quickly become scuffed and grubby.*

wool, 100 per cent synthetic fibre, or any conceivable blend of the two.

Don't let the different terms confuse you. To help identify carpet weights and suitability, manufacturers and retailers label all carpets with guidelines to their usage, fibre content and durability, so you can check that you're choosing the right carpet for the right room.

For any area where the floor is going to be in constant use – where looks and a long life really matter – the best option is a mix of 80 per cent pure wool and 20 per cent man-made fibres. This combines the natural quality, resilience and good looks of wool with just enough synthetic fibre to strengthen it.

Carpets with a higher proportion of synthetic fibre – right down to 100 per cent nylon or polyester – will be good enough for low-use   35

JOINS AND JUNCTIONS: WHERE ROOMS MEET
Before making any final decisions, remember that each floor area is going to meet another somewhere, even if it's just the hall or landing it leads on to. Different rooms, especially kitchens and bathrooms, will have different flooring requirements, so you'll need to think about how these surfaces are going to look next to one another at the junction points – in doorways, for instance, or at the top and bottom of a staircase. The join itself can be tidied up by a threshold strip, a metal or plastic strip which is nailed down to hide the raw edges and prevent them from being scuffed or frayed. But you will also want to make sure that adjoining colours, patterns and textures don't clash.

Herringbone

Diamond

Chequers

areas like bedrooms, and for use underneath rugs. If you've got a large area to cover, you can do it very economically with a cheap man-made carpet in a plain colour as a background to loose rugs and mats. But if it's going to get any sort of consistent heavy wear, remember that it will start to show its age very quickly. It won't clean as well as wool, and the static attracts more dirt, so it can get grubby and greasy very quickly and end up being a false economy.

Bathrooms need special waterproof carpet, so if you can't bear to step out of a warm bath on to a cold floor, make sure that you choose a carpet that has a waterproof backing.

Fitting and laying carpet Laying carpet isn't a DIY job, so leave it to the professionals. Remember that your carpet will also need a good underfelt or underlay: this will act as a shock absorber, and increase the springiness and longevity of the carpet.

Natural Matting

Coir, sisal, seagrass and jute can give the same all-over effect as a plain carpet, but with a rugged, serviceable feel that's closer to the look of natural wood and provides a good base for loose rugs – neutral and non-slip. Much more practical and sophisticated than old-style rush matting, the new natural floors are tighter-woven and harder-wearing. They can be bought by length (like carpet) or as tiles, with a latex backing, and are easy to keep clean with regular vacuuming.

Some of them come with a definite design

▲ *Natural floorcoverings come in a variety of weaves, such as herringbone, diamond patterns and chequers, adding a sense of pattern to the neutral colours.*

worked into the weave, such as herringbone or chequerboard. Traditionally sold in their natural range of neutral shades – from very light blond through greens and golds to richer russet tones – they are available in a variety of dyes nowadays, so if you like the practicality but find the natural tone rather too functional, you can choose from a range of colours including deep blues, greens, ochres and terracottas, or select one that has a neutral base with coloured fibres running through it.

Coir and sisal are the most hard-wearing of the natural floors. They're not cheap, but if you are choosing flooring for halls and stairs, they will match the price of the sort of tough-quality carpet you would need to do the same job. Seagrass is slightly cheaper and extremely resistant to dirt and stains. Jute is the cheapest of the four, and softest to the touch. It's not as hardy, but the softness makes it ideal for bedrooms and sitting rooms which don't get so much wear.

Basic rush matting is still a good standby, but it

▶ *Painted boards make one of the cheapest and most effective floors, and are a good way of covering up stains and knots in old wood. A matt or low-sheen paint finish is best for this – gloss will look uncomfortably shiny. Seal it with clear matt varnish to protect the surface.*

needs more looking after. It will collect dirt and let dust through, so you need to lift it regularly and sweep the floor underneath. The advantage is that it is available in squares which can be sewn together to cover as small or as large an area as you want. Because it is loose-laid, you can take it with you when you move, or use it as an extra layer when needed – for example, in a hall or passageway.

HARD FLOORS

Hard floors fall into three main categories: wood and wood-effect laminates; ceramic tiles; and flexible flooring materials such as vinyl, linoleum and cork.

Wood

A plain wood floor combines a marvellously uncluttered feel with the warmth of the natural grain. This sort of floor looks good in halls, sitting rooms and bedrooms. If your existing floorboards are in good condition, your cheapest option is to sand and varnish them, or leave them as they are and paint them. If you want to put down new wood, you can choose from a variety of manufactured planking and blocks. They generally come either as parquet blocks (with the wood set in geometric patterns to give a mosaic effect) or in long planks which slot together on a tongue-and-groove basis. Both of these can be laid over an existing floor as long as it is reasonably level.

Whatever you go for, always take time to choose the right colour and finish. Remember that wood is only brown in children's paintings – in reality it can be gold, red, or almost purple, so you need to consider your furnishing colours and choose a floor that will match.

SANDING WOOD FLOORS

The only real expense involved in DIY floor sanding is hiring a sander. You'll need a drum sander for the main floor area, a smaller rotary sander to tackle the edges, and three grades of paper – coarse, medium and then fine for a good finish. The floor needs to be levelled and any gaps filled before you start to sand. Make sure that any protruding nail heads are either removed or hammered back below floor level. Nail loose and warped boards down firmly, and fill gaps between boards with strips of wood wedged into place and planed off. Obvious nail indentations can be hidden with a dab of wood filler.

■ Sand across the floor diagonally first, using coarse sandpaper and overlapping each row by a couple of inches. Then change to medium-grade paper and sand along the length of the boards, in the direction of the grain. When you get to the far end of each row, raise the sanding

▼ *New wood floors can be laid using blocks or tongue-and-groove planks that slot together.*

▲ *If you want to add more decoration to a plain wood floor, stencil or paint a simple border around the edge.*

belt as you change direction. Sand along the length again with fine-grade paper and then complete the room by sanding the edges with the rotary sander.

■ Sweep the sanded floor well and wipe it down with white spirit so that it is completely dust-free before you varnish it. Varnishes can be clear, letting the natural tone show through, or coloured in a variety of wood shades. You can also buy special wood stains which add a layer of translucent colour – such as green or blue – without covering up the grain of the wood.

Ceramic Tiles

Ceramic tiles provide a good-looking, hard-wearing floor that is waterproof and easy to clean. They can be used to create a vast range of effects, from a plain run of one colour to a decorative pattern of different colours, shapes and sizes. They're extremely useful for floors in kitchens, which will need washing frequently; in bathrooms, which need to be waterproof; and in halls, which need to be tough and, again, easy to clean. The disadvantages, however, are that they can be cold and noisy to walk on, and breakables dropped on them are unlikely to survive!

Tiled floors need to be laid on a completely flat surface – and on one that is strong enough to hold their weight. If you're planning to lay them in an upstairs room, or an upper-storey flat, get a surveyor to check the structural suitability of the floor first.

Glazed tiles Glazed floor tiles look more or less like ceramic wall tiles, and they work on the same principle – stuck down with a special floor tile adhesive, and then grouted to seal the gaps. But they are thicker and are fired at a higher temperature, to make them virtually unbreakable. (Don't try laying wall tiles as a budget alternative: they aren't strong enough.) They need a heavy-duty tile cutter, and you're likely to waste a number of tiles while attempting to cut them, so unless you're practised at this job it's better to leave it to a professional.

Glazed ceramic tiles are available in black and

◄ *If you like the idea of ceramic floor tiles but are put off by the cost, stick to plain tiles in one or two colours for the main area, with decorative tiles providing a border.*

▲ *Terracotta tiles can be laid in a variety of patterns, and are available cut to different shapes so that smaller decorative pieces can be worked into the design.*

white and a host of other plain colours, or patterned with a decorative design – often hand-painted, giving a slightly rustic effect. Plain colours may differ slightly in shade from box to box, so check all your boxes before the tiles are laid. If there is any variation, it's a good idea to mix tiles from different boxes so that the variation is random and not concentrated in one area of the floor.

Contrasting plain tiles can be used to make a chequered floor. The traditional black and white chessboard pattern always looks good, or you could try other combinations such as blue and yellow, or green and white, to match your furnishings.

Decorated tiles can be very expensive, but you can create a very effective floor by using a few small decorative insets in a run of plain tiles. And small glazed decorated tiles look marvellous as insets in a floor of larger unglazed quarry or terracotta tiles.

Quarry and terracotta tiles The unglazed, earth-coloured tiles that you tend to find in farmhouse kitchens and Mediterranean homes. Because they are all terracotta-*coloured*, the two terms are often assumed to be interchangeable. In fact terracotta tiles are made literally from pure baked clay and are more expensive, whereas quarry tiles include a high proportion of silica (quartz). Quarries are fired at a higher temperature, which gives them a less porous surface that looks smoother than true terracotta. Quarries are tougher and more practical, but terracotta offers a greater range of colours – from very light creamy shades to deep red browns. Terracotta tiles need to be sealed to make their surface resistant to staining from water and grease.

Terracotta tiles are available in larger sizes than standard ceramics, and also cut into hexagonal and octagonal shapes, and small lozenges (diamond shapes) which will fit between octagonal tiles as insets. (This is where you can use decorative glazed insets if you prefer.)

Flexible Flooring

The big advantage of the floors in the 'flexible' category is that most of them are fairly easy to lay on a DIY basis (the exception is linoleum). Waterproof and practical to clean, they are an obvious choice for kitchens, bathrooms and utility areas.

Linoleum Lino went out of fashion with the introduction of man-made vinyls, but it has regained popularity because of its hard-wearing surface and also because of its surprisingly natural make-up. It consists of a mixture of cork, wood, linseed oil and resins, all compressed on to a jute or hessian backing. The linseed oil means that it actually gets tougher as it ages, but it can crack easily when still soft, which is why it needs professional laying. Lino comes in a wide range of plain colours, marbled effects and patterns; and in sheet form or tiles – so it can provide a plain

▶ *Terracotta tiles are ideal for halls, utility rooms and wherever you want an attractive, washable surface. Terracotta that has been frostproofed looks good outside as well as inside, so using it in a room that leads out to a patio or garden is a good way of linking the two areas. In this garden room, small ceramic tiles have been inset at intervals to add decoration.*

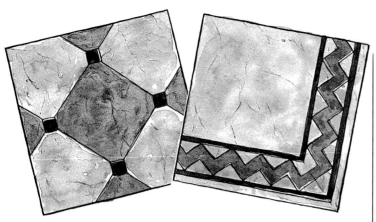

▲ *Lino and vinyl can be cut into different shapes to make clever patterns imitating classical tiles and mosaics.*

background or a chequerboard pattern, and can also be used to make a decorative floor inset with different shapes and motifs.

Vinyls Available in different grades, can be flat or cushioned, and is sold either in sheet form or as adhesive-backed tiles. Bathrooms can get away with the thinner quality, while halls and kitchens ideally need a thicker grade or a cushioned vinyl to keep the floor comfortable and quiet underfoot. The range of colours and patterns is very versatile, including imitations of traditional tiled and mosaic floors, and even of natural materials such as marble, granite and terracotta (very useful if you like the look, but not the price or the chilly surface).

Cork Cork tiles are a good compromise between the practical, waterproof, manufactured floorings and the natural look and warmer feel of wood. Very economical, they are easy to lay and provide a natural insulating layer (good for bathrooms, where wood isn't practical). They aren't as durable as vinyl or lino, and must be sealed to prevent them rotting and crumbling around the edges. Some cork tiles come pre-sealed; unsealed tiles will need a coat of clear vinyl or polyurethane once they are laid.

Rugs and Runners
Loose rugs give you the best of all worlds — pattern, colour and comfort underfoot, but in movable quantities so that you can change the effect as often as you want and update it to match new furnishings. Rugs and mats are a godsend wherever you need to cover up a floor that doesn't quite come up to scratch.

Non-slip backing is essential wherever loose rugs or carpets are used on a hard floor.

DESIGNING YOUR OWN RUGS

Simple, contemporary-style rugs are easy to make by insetting panels of carpet offcuts into a plain backing colour. Choosing exactly the colours you want and working out your own original pattern, you can design a rug specifically to match a particular room or colour scheme.

■ Offcuts are available at bargain rates from carpet shops. Short-pile or velour carpet offcuts work best for this technique, but they must be rubber- or foam-backed. You'll need a large piece for the background colour and smaller scraps to make the inset panels. Or you could make a pair of mirror-image rugs by cutting

Make use of carpet offcuts to design your own exclusive rug by insetting panels into a background piece. This pair make a mirror image set, because the cutouts from one have been fitted into the other.

out identical shapes from two pieces of carpet and then swapping them – black shapes on a white background and white shapes on a black background, for instance.

■ Work out your pattern on paper first. Geometric and straight-edged shapes are the easiest to cut out, as you can use a ruler or plank of wood as a guide to cut against. Look for useful items that will make rigid templates for other shapes: upside-down flower pots or metal waste bins can be cut around if you want a circle.

■ Lay the main colour on a large piece of hardboard as a cutting surface. Cut the shapes carefully out of it, using a Stanley knife or trimming blade, and then cut matching shapes from the other offcuts. Fit these into the spaces, then turn the rug over and tape the joins with double-sided carpet tape.

■ To back the rug, cut a piece of carpet felt to fit, leaving a slight border so that you can trim it exactly when it's in place. Paste it with a strong water-based adhesive, lay it over the back of the rug and press it in place. The tape will help keep it in position until the glue has dried completely. Then trim the backing.

PAINTING A FLOOR

Painted floors are cheap and effective. Painting a floor is a good alternative to sanding floorboards if the quality or grain of the wood isn't good enough to be exposed, but it can be just as easily achieved on a plain concrete base. You'll want a surface you can clean marks off, but gloss paint – the usual choice for woodwork – has too high a sheen for floors, so the best option is vinyl matt or silk emulsion sealed with clear matt varnish (check with your retailer that the varnish is tough enough).

The best thing about a painted floor is that you can design it exactly as you want, and repaint over the top when you get tired of it.

■ A chequerboard design is one of the simplest and most effective, suggestive of traditional tiles. It can be worked square-on, like a chessboard, or set on a diagonal – the latter is easier

if the room isn't completely square, as none of the lines will be parallel to the walls.

■ Prime the floor first using a wood primer or concrete sealer, depending on the surface.

■ Try out your colours on a sample patch of floor first (add a coat of varnish over the top as well, to make sure that this doesn't alter the shade).

■ Outline the pattern with masking tape to get a defined edge as you paint. If you're using one light and one dark colour, you can save time by painting a coat of the lighter colour all over the floor, and then marking out squares on it to add your second colour over the top. If the two shades are nearer in density this won't be possible, and you'll have to mark out the squares on the primer before adding any colour.

■ When you're happy with the effect (you may want more than one coat of at least one of your colours), let it dry thoroughly and sweep the floor clear of fluff and dust.

■ Finally varnish with clear matt varnish. The more coats you can manage, the better, as this will give a good seal and help to stop the pattern wearing. But don't be impatient – it's important to let each coat dry before applying the next.

▲ *Chequered floors can be created with tiles or paintwork. For a room where the walls aren't quite parallel, diagonal chequers are best. If you want a squared-up chessboard effect, design the pattern so that you finish with a row of complete tiles along each side, and then add plain border tiles in one colour to complete the edges.*

43

Windows

Windows are a natural focal point and, in modern houses particularly, they can take the place of a fireplace or chimney breast in giving architectural interest to a blank wall. Curtains, blinds and shutters come in all shapes and sizes, to suit all kinds of window, and some windows look good enough to need barely any dressing at all.

The two main elements to consider with a window are the amount of light it lets in and the amount of privacy it gives you. Remember that the more you get of one, the less you'll have of the other. Rooms where you spend a lot of time – living rooms and kitchens, for instance – will generally benefit from a good supply of light, and you probably won't feel it necessary to keep the window heavily screened unless your house fronts a busy street. In bedrooms and bathrooms, on the other hand, light and privacy need to be carefully balanced.

The view framed by the window needs to be taken into account too. If there's a pleasant outlook, you'll want a window treatment that makes the most of it. And a less attractive view can be just as effectively hidden or disguised by careful use of curtains and blinds.

You also need to think about the structure of the window itself. How big is it and what shape? If it's small, you want to be careful you don't obscure it by vast quantities of fabric so that it doesn't let in any light at all. To make it look larger and let in maximum light, fix a long pole so that the curtains can be pulled right back on either side. If it's an awkward shape, on the other hand, or set in an awkward position, you can use a clever window treatment to change the shape visually or improve the proportions of the room. A tall, thin window can be widened by fitting a deep pelmet with wide-set curtains. If the window is set towards a corner, you can balance the proportions of the room by hanging a single curtain on the side nearest the adjacent wall – this will give the effect of bringing the window further into the room.

CURTAINS

Curtains are as versatile as the fabric you make them from, and can be adapted to create a host of different effects. They can be cut to any length and trimmed to any shape. They can be lined, unlined or completely sheer. Don't be put off by the thought of fiddly pleats, gathers and layers of lining: some of the most effective window treatments are the simplest to put together.

The fabric you use – its weight and texture as well as colour and pattern – will depend on the style of curtain you want. As long as the fabric has the right weight and drape to create the desired effect, and your heading and fixings are strong enough to support it, you can use more or less any fabric. If the fabric is very light – net or

---

▶ *A single lace panel provides the ideal curtain for this bedroom window, screening it from view without blocking out the light. It's a narrow window, so the idea was to avoid obscuring it with too much fabric. The slim rail set inside the recess shows off the interesting shape of the recess itself, and a paintwork border takes the place of traditional side curtains and pelmet to frame the whole effect. The curtain itself involves the minimum of sewing. The sides have their own scalloped edging, and the top just needs a basic hem. Brass clips catch it on to the curtain rings, so there are no gathers or heading tape to worry about, and it can be hooked to one side with a ribbon or tie-back to give it a little more shape wihout leaving the room exposed to view.*

muslin, for instance – weighted tape sewn into the hems of the curtains will make them hang better.

The key is never to skimp on the amount of fabric: you'll achieve a more luxurious effect with a quantity of cheap fabric than with a more modest length of something expensive. Lightweight dress fabrics are often cheaper than materials designed specifically for furnishing, and will be perfectly good for a small, simple curtain. And you should make the most of large, ready-made panels of fabric such as bed covers, table cloths and sheeting where you can – as well as saving on cost, you won't have to stitch extra widths together!

Remember that an obvious repeat pattern will need more skill to make up, and you'll also have to buy more fabric to match the widths. The easiest fabrics to work with are plain colours, all-over random patterns, and simple checks and stripes, especially if they are the same on both sides, like gingham or ticking, so that you don't need a lining.

Poles and Tracks
Flat aluminium or nylon tracks are designed specifically for traditional gathered curtains, and come fitted with a row of sliding runners into which you slot the curtain hooks. This is a good solution where there isn't room for a pole – if you want to hang the curtain inside the window recess, for instance – or where a pole would look

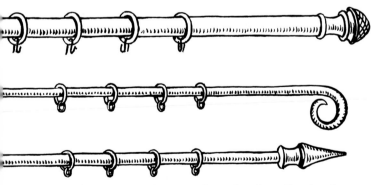

▲ *Curtain poles range from slim 1-cm (½-in) rails to sturdy 6-cm (2½-in) wooden poles, with a variety of decorative finials.*

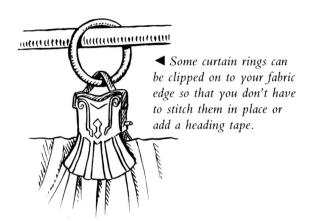

◀ *Some curtain rings can be clipped on to your fabric edge so that you don't have to stitch them in place or add a heading tape.*

too dominant and unbalance the effect of the window.

Poles and rails – wooden, brass or wrought iron – give the window a more finished look. They come in a variety of diameters from about 1 cm (½ in) to about 6 cm (2½ in), and can be plain or ornate, with extra decoration added by the finials, or end pieces. Because this sort of fixing makes the curtain hang a little way out from the wall, it is much better than a flat track for windows with a protruding surround.

Make sure that you buy the right length of pole for the window. Standard lengths are available from furnishing departments and DIY stores, or you can have special orders cut to size. It needs to extend quite a few centimetres either side of the window to balance its proportions and take the pulled-back curtain.

Remember to calculate the position of your curtain heading carefully before you fix the pole or rail to the wall. If the top of the curtain is going to hang some way below the pole (for example, on big hoop curtain rings), make sure that it will be high enough to conceal the window frame.

Measuring Up
Curtains can be cropped to rest neatly on the sill, or end a little way below it – for instance, at radiator height – or they can be floor-length. For a sense of real opulence they can even be made with a foot or so of excess fabric that collects in luxurious puddles beneath the window.

Remember that you don't have to cover the whole window at all. Hanging the curtain from a pole fixed half-way or two-thirds of the way up is a clever method of making a tall window look less dominant.

The width of fabric you need will depend on how full you want the curtain to be. Standard heading tapes require between one and a half and two and a half times the curtain width (see the notes on individual tapes, this page). These calculations are for a pair of curtains in plain or random-patterned fabric:

1 Measure the width of the track or pole – not the window. To allow for any gathers, multiply this figure according to the type of tape you're using. Now divide the total by the width of the fabric you've chosen. (Most furnishing fabric is 137 cm (54 in) wide.)

2 Round this up to the next whole figure (unless it's only slightly over a whole figure – that is, less than 0.1 – in which case you can round it down). This gives you the number of widths of fabric you'll need for two curtains.

▲ *The space above a window is worth making use of and can add to the effect of the window dressing. A pole with an integral shelf on top provides an instant curtain fixing for a simple window and gives you a display area to make the heading more decorative at the same time.*

3 Now measure the drop from the pole or track to the level you want the curtain to hang. Add 30 cm (12 in) to allow for hems and headings, and multiply by the number of fabric widths calculated above to find the total length of fabric you need to buy.

Gathered Curtains

Traditional gathered curtains consist of panels of fabric measuring between one and a half and two and a half times the width of the area they are covering. Special tape sewn into the heading is threaded with cord which gathers the fabric to the required width when pulled. Different tape produces different types of gather or pleat, some using up more fabric width than others, so you need to decide how full you want your curtains to be as well as what you want the heading to look like.

Standard gathered heading tape Quite narrow – about 2.5 cm (1 in) wide – and gathers the curtain into a basic ruffled effect. You'll need one and a half to two times the fabric width. The gathers aren't deep enough to make the curtain fall in formal folds or pleats, so this tape is best for small, lightweight curtains, or where the top will be covered by a pelmet or valance. It's most often used with a standard plastic track. If you want to use it with a decorative pole, make sure that you fix the tape slightly below the edge of the curtain, so that the hooks don't show over the top when it's hung in place.

Pencil-pleat heading tape Gathers the curtain into neat pencil-width pleats so that the fabric hangs in fuller folds – the fabric needs to be two and a quarter to two and a half times the curtain width you want to end up with. Because the heading itself is deeper, it gives the curtain a more finished effect, and if you use the lower row of hook loops, the hooks will be hidden below the top of the curtain.

Pinch-pleat heading Gathers the curtain into groups of pleats – most commonly triple – with a stretch of ungathered fabric between each group. Like pencil-pleat heading, it gives a formal, finished effect, but the pleats are quite

47

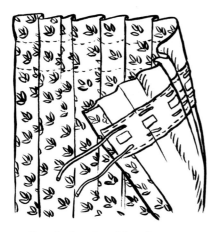

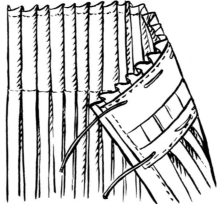

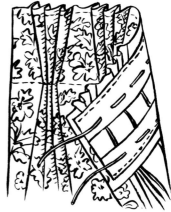

Standard gathered heading tape.　　*Pencil-pleat heading tape.*　　*Triple pinch-pleat heading tape.*

subtle and don't take up much fullness: you'll need twice the fabric width. Again, you can use the lower row of hook loops to make sure that the hooks are kept out of sight.

Quick-sew Curtains

The newer trend is for a simpler style of heading, often with the fabric just tied or threaded on to a pole, or wrapped around it. With so many good-looking tie-backs and hold-backs available, the curtains don't even have to draw in the conventional sense – the fabric can simply be hooked back out of the way.

Curtains like these tend not to be so full, with the advantage that they use up less fabric, and –

best of all – they often require little sewing beyond the side seams and hems. They also make more of a feature of the pole itself, so it's a good chance to try out some of the decorative poles. Quick to make and very adaptable, they are particularly good for small rooms where too much fabric would look over-fussy.

The simplicity of these treatments lends itself to understated fabrics like checks and stripes or plain undyed cottons and calicos, but you can vary the effect to make it as functional or as decorative as you like. A more elaborately patterned fabric such as a floral print can look very effective offset by a simple heading instead of the more traditional frills and flounces.

To shade a large window that gets plenty of light, or to provide privacy without obscuring the light entirely, plain cotton muslin or calico can be draped in a double length over the pole. You'll probably need to stitch two fabric widths together, but apart from that the only sewing necessary is to hem the two raw edges. The fabric itself is not expensive, so allow yourself the luxury of extra quantity – you can knot the two lengths at window-sill level to give the effect of a huge tassel. Or just tie a loose knot in the foreground length so that the other one screens the window in a neat panel (weighted tape sewn into the hems will give it a better drape).

◄ *Swathes of muslin looped around a pole and hanging in drapes at one or both sides of a window look luxurious and need very little sewing — you just have to sew the lengths of fabric together to form one long train. (To calculate the amount needed, add the width of the pole to twice the height of the pole from the floor. Now add another pole-and-a-half width to allow for the folds and swags and leave you with a generous sweep of fabric where it meets the floor.) Find the centre of the fabric length and loop it over the centre of the pole to give you a starting point. You can either wind the fabric in the same direction right along the pole, or create a symmetrical effect by winding in opposite directions.*

◄ *A lightweight or loose-woven fabric can be threaded on to a pole itself if you stitch a deep hem along the top. If there's too much fabric for the curtain head to gather easily, you can counter this by bunching the curtains into tie-backs lower down.*

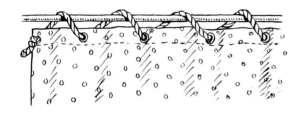

► *Fabric tabs stitched into the top of a curtain to give a 'battlement' effect form instant curtain rings and can be looped straight on to the pole.*

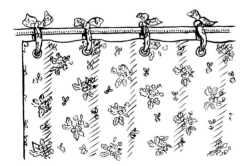

Brass eyelets inset along the top of a curtain in place of traditional hooks or rings have a practical, nautical feel and are great for a number of effects. The simplest is to thread the curtain itself on to a slim pole, such as a wrought-iron design. Or you can continue the nautical theme and use plain rope or cord to lash the curtain loosely on to the pole. And the whole effect can be prettied up into something much less functional if you use this sort of simple eyelet heading for a floral curtain, tying it on to a decorative pole with ribbons or strips of matching fabric looped through each eyelet and finished in a bow.

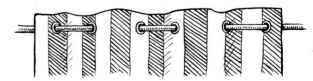

49

To Line or not to Line?

Lining your curtains traditionally makes them look more finished from outside the window. Formal curtains and heavy fabrics hang better if they are lined, and lining will improve the insulating effect and protect the main fabric from fading in the sun. Many of the simpler curtain effects shown here don't really need a lining at all, but if you can afford the extra fabric, they're a great way of adding contrasting colour, pattern and trimming. By using two inexpensive fabrics together – one as the curtain and the other as the lining – you can turn them into a double-sided curtain that looks richer and more luxurious.

MAKING A SIMPLE LINING

The easiest lining to make is simply stitched to the main curtain down the sides so that it forms a backing. Standard cotton sateen lining is cheap and practical and comes in a wide range of colours. If you're using any other sort of fabric, remember to check that the two fabrics have compatible washing or cleaning requirements – for example, they are both dry-cleanable, or both machine-washable at the same temperature – you don't want to have to take them apart again.

To measure up for a basic lining, you'll need the lining fabric to be 23 cm (9 in) shorter and 13 cm (5 in) narrower than the main curtain, so that the curtain edges fold around the lining slightly at the back, and the lining finishes 5 cm (2 in) above the lower edge of the curtain.

◀ *A small window set in a deep recess needs careful dressing to brighten up what could be a gloomy, cell-like feature. Contrasting colours and fabrics have been used here to open up the effect. The double-sided curtains are gathered on to hinged rails which swing out from the window, keeping the window itself completely clear and at the same time lining the sides of the recess to give them a little more interest. The deep sill is made the most of as a display shelf, and a matching wallpaper border frames the surround to make the whole window look bigger.*

1 Stitch the curtain fabric widths together to the required size and press the seams open. Do the same with the lining widths. Lay the lining fabric on top of the main fabric, right sides together and with the top of the lining fabric 8 cm (3 in) below the top of the main fabric.
2 Align one pair of curtain and lining edges and pin them together down the length of the lining fabric. Now do the same with the opposite pair of edges (you'll need to pull the lining across because of the extra curtain width). Machine-stitch the edges, starting at the top and stopping 5 cm (2 in) above the lower edge of the lining. Then turn up the lining in a 2.5-cm (1-in) double hem to the wrong side.
3 Press the side seams open, then turn the curtain the right way out. Lay it flat so that the lining panel is centred, with equal margins of curtain down either side, and press the side folds. Turn down the top edge of the curtain so that it encloses the raw lining edge, and attach your curtain heading. Finally, turn up the bottom of the curtain in a 5-cm (2-in) double hem and press lightly.

Loose Linings

Some curtain hooks are designed with an extra loop at the bottom on to which you can hang a second, lighter-weight curtain to act as a lining. The advantage of a completely detachable lining is that you can remove it for washing separately, or store it away altogether in warmer weather when you don't need the extra insulation. And you can change the effect by unhooking the lining and replacing it with a different fabric.

Try hanging a coloured lining behind a lace or sheer curtain so that the colour shows through in the sunlight. Or gather the curtain into a tie-back to leave the lining layer screening the window – a sheer lining will act like a traditional net curtain, while a more decorative one can give a rather opulent feel.

Once you've got the principle of two layers working together, you can add all sorts of details and effects to make the most of it.

51

TIE-BACKS AND TRIMMINGS

As well as keeping curtains in place and out of the way, tie-backs and hold-backs are an instant way of giving them line and shape – defining the window and catching the fabric into attractive folds.

Simple fabric tie-backs can be cut from material to match or contrast with the curtains themselves, stiffened with interfacing and finished with brass rings to hook them on to the walls at either side of the window. Use a flexible measuring tape to experiment with the best size of tie-back for the bulk of the curtain: this will give you the basic span of the tie-back, which you can then shape or trim to the design you want.

You can also rustle up tie-backs from cords, braids and spare fabric remnants. Scarves and dressing-gown cords complete with their own tassels provide instant trimming. Use plain nautical rope to offset crisp cottons, ticking and gingham. A single curtain at a door or a large window can simply be buckled to one side with a leather belt or even a length of chain for a heavier, chunker effect.

Hold-backs do the same job with a rigid fitting – usually a hook or knob attached to the wall. Often rather formal/ornate and usually sold in

▲ *A couple of decorative hold-backs or brass knobs set on either side of the window can be draped with a length of muslin or other lightweight fabric – even a long scarf or shawl – to form an instant curtain and pelmet effect with no pole or track needed.*

▲ *A pelmet or valance is a neat way to finish a curtain heading – and will hide a multitude of sins. For a really simple curtain effect, attach a wooden batten to the wall in place of a curtain track or pole. Make basic single-width curtains and attach them to the batten with strips of Velcro. Use tie-backs to pull them to the sides of the window, and fit a simple pelmet to neaten the heading.* ▼

▶ *Two different fabrics have been used here to create the simplest possible curtain. Sewn back to back, they make a luxurious double-sided curtain that can just be looped over the wooden pole. You can adjust an effect like this to hang at any length you want and give a different drape. The lop-sided look here keeps the corner of the room clear for the chair, with the fabric bunched into plain tie-backs.*

Dressing-gown cord

Leather belt

Knotted scarf

Plain rope

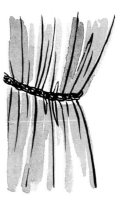
Bicycle chain

▲ *Tie-backs give your curtains a better line and are a quick solution for dress curtains that don't pull aside at the top.*

◄ *Doorknobs and plaster mouldings can be used as rigid curtain hold-backs for a more formal effect.*

pairs, they can end up costing more than the curtains themselves, but you can improvize very effective alternatives from decorative doorknobs and handles, brackets, plaster mouldings and other architectural details.

BLINDS

Blinds can be made of fabric, paper, nylon, wood or various other materials. Fabric blinds can be as decorative as curtains, but because the fabric itself is collected at the top rather than the sides of the window, it doesn't get in the way of other furnishings or of activity in the room. Basic kits to make them are inexpensive to buy, easy to use and come with full instructions and fabric measuring guidelines. Plastic and wood Venetian slatted designs are particularly useful for kitchens and bathrooms as they are neat, uncluttered and practical to clean. And simple paper roller blinds can be used either on their own or as a supplement to curtains.

In general, blinds obscure less light than

curtains by keeping the bulk of the window clear, but if you live in a basement flat, remember that the light will be coming in at a downward-slanted angle, and by obscuring the top of the window you could be shutting it out. On the other hand, you'll be well protected from prying eyes at pavement level, so it's really a question of which is more important to you – daylight or privacy.

Roller Blinds

Roller blinds are the easiest to make and the simplest in style. They use up the minimum amount of fabric – stretched flat across the window with no pleats or tucks – and take up the minimum of space, rolling up into a slim cylinder at the top of the window. If the window is narrow, you may be able to get away with using a single width of fabric so that the selvedges form the side edges and don't need turning or binding (although a contrasting edging can be added for effect if you want).

You will need to use a firm fabric which rolls up easily – your fabric retailer will be able to advise you. Roller blind kits are sold in standard sizes, but the dowelling rod around which the fabric rolls up can be cut to fit your window. Roller blinds are best fitted *inside* the window recess so that the sides of the recess provide a home for the fixings. Ready-made roller blinds in bamboo and rush are also available, giving an effect a little more like a slatted Venetian blind, as they let light filter through the weave.

Roman Blinds

Roman blinds are simple and, again, economical on fabric, but instead of rolling, the fabric is pulled up into deep folds, giving a slightly more decorative effect. The blind is hung from a rigid batten, and the folds can be stiffened by battens too, or left so that the folds are softer and less formal. The folds are created by threading the pull cords through loops at regular intervals down the length of the blind – the wider the interval, the deeper the fold.

▶ *Slatted shutters let in wonderful dappled light and are good for bathrooms and kitchens where you don't want lots of fabric getting in the way.*

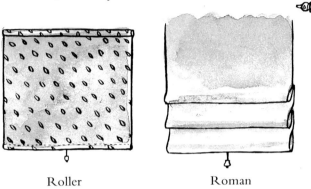

Roller   Roman

▲ *Plain roller and roman blinds provide neat, tailored curtain dressing.*

▲ *Shutters can be fitted to work like curtains, hung on a pole so that they simply pull back to the sides of the window. You'll need the pole to extend far enough each side to take the shutters when they're pulled back. Brass or steel loops are screwed into the top edge of each shutter at the left and right corners, to hang it on to the pole.*

Austrian Blinds

Austrian blinds are much fuller and more dressy: a good choice for a window where you'd really like gathered curtains but feel they'd get in the way. The fullness comes from a series of tapes running vertically through the blind so that the fabric gathers into ruches when it's pulled up.

Festoon Blinds

Even more luxurious than Austrian blinds, festoons work on the same ruched principle, but using more fabric, so they look very gathered and flouncy even when let down to their fullest extent.

SHUTTERS

Wooden shutters can take the place of curtains or blinds altogether. Older buildings may have original shutters still intact – it's worth checking to see whether old shutters have been boarded up

into your window surround. Solid shutters like these are excellent insulators in cold weather, as well as being a good security measure.

Louvred shutters that fold back at the sides give more of a colonial or Mediterranean effect. Some are designed with adjustable louvres so that you can vary the angle of the slats to control the amount of light you let in – from a horizontal position making the openings as wide as possible, to a more shaded angle that sheds a wonderful dappled light indoors.

If you like the idea of shutters but feel the room is too small for them to fold out comfortably, you can cheat by fitting false shutters that don't actually move at all. Fixed to the wall on either side of the window, they will frame it rather like curtains, making it look wider and giving it better proportions.

Halls and Entrances

Behind every front door is the beginning of a new story. Like the first page of a book, this is the image that will present the first impression of your home. What do you want it to convey? Elegance? Comfort? Familiarity? Drama? The first few steps inside will establish a distinct idea in your visitors' minds, and set the tone for the rooms beyond.

The entrance to your home has to fulfil three functions at once. It must act as a practical arrival point: somewhere people can leave coats and luggage without disrupting the living area too much. It also needs to play the same role in a psychological sense – extending a welcome into an unfamiliar setting or reinforcing the warmth of a familiar one. And it should stamp an identity on your home and give it a decorative starting point for any continuing theme.

Remember that the hall is a room in itself – don't just treat it as a transit area. Although it will have to link the rooms that lead off it, you want it to have a character of its own.

COLOUR AND STYLE

Most halls are little more than a passageway or lobby with individual rooms leading off it, so you need to choose a colour scheme that can cope with the decorative problems of small size and awkward shape. The simplest way is to stick to a single background colour. Plain painted walls are the best option here (especially if, like many halls, yours has corners that are tricky to paper around).

Opening up the Space with Light Colours
Pale colours will reflect any available light and make a small room feel bigger, but remember that they vary from warm to cold, so be careful of the effect you are creating.

Cool greens, blues and lemon yellows will all achieve a good feeling of space, but unless your hall gets a lot of natural daylight you may find them rather *too* cold. In this case, go for soft pinks and peaches or sunnier yellows, which will be warmer and make the initial impression a more welcoming one.

Whites, off-whites and creams are the easiest of all, and have the added bonus of providing you with a neutral background to link whatever colour schemes you decide on for adjoining rooms. White can feel rather stark and clinical as an all-over effect, so look for a shade with a hint of warmer colour mixed in. Or, if you're keen to keep the effect completely neutral, try a softer ivory white, which has all the advantages of bright white but provides the slightly richer quality of a genuine cream.

▶ *This house had the classic hall problems of high ceiling, narrow walls and very little light. Fitting glass panels into the door immediately improved things. The walls were then lined with wood panelling up to shoulder height, which automatically brought the height of the ceiling down, disguising the stairwell looming above. Painting the door, walls, ceiling and staircase in a single colour creates a more spacious effect. When the floorboards were uncovered, they were found to be laid crossways across the hall instead of down its length. This helps make the space look wider and less like a corridor.*

56

The problem with a hall is that the ceiling is usually the same height as in the other rooms, but the walls are considerably closer together. The result of this is often a tall, thin, 'chimney' effect which feels uncomfortable and looks unwelcoming. So do what you can to lower the ceiling and open up the walls, and make the most of the available sources of light.

● A dado rail half-way up the wall, or a wallpaper or painted border added at dado-rail level, will break up the expanse of wall height, making the walls feel less tall and the room wider.

● A picture rail, or a border at picture-rail level, will visually lower the ceiling. Use a lighter paint colour than on the rest of the walls for the area above the rail and the ceiling itself, so that the ceiling appears to continue into the walls and therefore looks wider – this will have the effect of pushing the walls apart visually.

● A narrow shelf fixed at picture-rail height will have the same effect, and books, ornaments – or a row of pretty plates – displayed at this level add a focal point that attracts the eye away from the real ceiling height.

● Paint radiators the same colour as the wall so that they blend into the background.

● Hall windows tend to be small, so don't over-dress them with a lot of fabric that obscures the light. Either make the window look bigger by hanging curtains that frame it, or think about neater shutters and blinds as an alternative.

● A plain, pale floor will widen the area – wood boards or a natural floor matting such as coir fitted wall to wall will look more spacious than a patterned carpet.

● Make use of mirrors to open up the space and reflect what light there is. A single large mirror can make the room feel twice the size.

 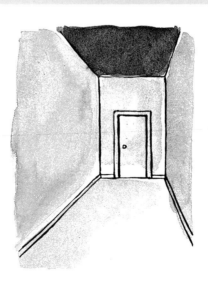

◀ *Adding a border or shelf around the walls will lower the ceiling height and make the ceiling area look wider so that it visually 'pushes' the walls apart. Wood floorboards laid across the hall will help to broaden the effect too.*
Another way to make a ceiling feel lower is to paint it a darker colour than the walls.

58

▲ *A hall isn't the most practical place for ornaments as they can easily be knocked over by people brushing past, but a high-level shelf can be used to display china or pictures.*

◄ *Make sure that small hall windows aren't obscured by lots of curtain fabric. Fit a single curtain that can be pulled back completely clear of the window to keep the area light.*

Using Bolder Colours to Make an Impression

If you're feeling more adventurous, you can go for a scheme that makes more of an impression from the outset.

Golds, ochres, corals and peaches – colours from the warmer end of the spectrum – will be welcoming and reassuring as you enter the house. These shades are also very responsive to whatever light is available, reflecting a soft glow that is restful on the eye and subtle as a background.

Deep blues, emerald greens, rich terracottas and other colours from the darker end of the spectrum will create a feeling of drama that gives your hall an instant sense of its own identity. This is an intriguing impression that invites people in and makes them want to see more.

Adding Pattern

Bold patterns are difficult to manage in a small hall, as they can confuse the eye and feel claustrophobic in a confined space. But if you don't want plain walls, a paper with a small motif or a subtle pattern on a light background can be just as effective in opening up the space.

Stripes can be turned to your advantage in a small space too. This is a good pattern for a low-ceilinged room. Aim for a broad, soft, vertical stripe – white with beige, yellow or a light pastel colour – which will add a subtle sense of pattern without being too strident. Or, if you want to use a darker colour, look for a very narrow pin stripe so that the colour appears as no more than a neat line against a cream or white background.

For more ideas see chapter on Colour and Pattern.

Opening up the Broader Picture

The hall is only the starting point, so try to lead the eye on towards other areas of interest. Accent colour is a great advantage here, because it can be used to link details in your hall with focus points in rooms beyond. If your sitting room opens off the hall, for instance, you can pick up the colour of the sitting-room walls to use for woodwork or curtain fabric in the hall, so that the hall has more sense of belonging to the rest of the house. At the same time, drawing the eye onwards into another room like this will also increase the sense of space in the hall by broadening the view of the immediate picture.

Stairs and Landings

If your hall also houses the foot of a staircase, you will want a scheme that can be maintained up the stairs and possibly along landings too, so bear this in mind before you opt for something that may be too much of a good thing if used in quantity. Because stairways and landings will also need plenty of light for safety and visibility, a pale, neutral colour scheme is a good option all round.

Hall lighting

Whatever the size of your hall, daylight will

probably be in short supply: in flats and apartments the area is frequently windowless, and even in a house you will rely on the additional light let through from other rooms and down the stairwell.

Hall lighting needs to be both practical and inviting, so it's important to get the level right. Don't go overboard with mood lighting here. You want to be able to see your guests clearly when they arrive and find your belongings easily when you're going out – and you also need the hall to bridge the gap between the indoor and outdoor worlds. What you want to aim for is a good overall level of background lighting, with side lamps or spots to vary the tone and illuminate practical things like mirrors and the telephone.

There are two ways in which lighting can help offset the box-like feel of a small hall. One is by deflecting attention away from the ceiling; the other is by illuminating the walls instead.

If the ceiling is high, a light that hangs some way below it will visually lower the effect and help to balance the proportions of the room. If the ceiling is not so high, think about fitting a few recessed downlighters. Because there isn't a visible fitting to attract the eye upwards, the ceiling won't seem so dominant.

For the walls, remember that a dappled surface – broken up by contrasting areas of light and shadow – will look softer and less oppressive than a flat one. Either fit recessed wall washers that cast a beam sideways on to the walls or go for wall brackets or uplighters. Ceramic uplighters can be painted the same colour as the wall itself so that they blend into the background.

Remember that all the wiring for wall lamps, downlighters and anything other than a central ceiling fitting must be in place before you start to decorate.

For more ideas see chapter on Lighting.

HALL FLOORS

An area that sees constant through traffic needs to be hard-wearing underfoot, especially if it is to withstand dirt and damp brought in from outside.

The easiest hall floor is one that is easy to sweep and wash, so hard floors are the most practical choice. As always, sanding and sealing any existing boards will be your cheapest option. Tiles will look good too. Terracotta or mosaic-laid ceramics may be affordable for a small area, or you can create your own pattern at less expense from vinyl or lino tiles.

Carpet will give a more welcoming feel underfoot, but make sure that you choose a hard-wearing fibre mix, and protect the areas that get most use with rugs. Natural coverings such as sisal and coir are more practical, and will be easier to budget for than carpet if you want to cover stairs and landings too. Their neutral shades are particularly useful in providing a background that won't clash with the colours of the rooms that lead off the hall.

Whatever flooring you opt for, a good doormat is an essential extra.

For more ideas see chapter on Floors.

HALL FURNITURE

If your hall is short on space, it's the last place where you want to install unnecessary furniture. But the beauty of well-designed hall furniture is that it actually saves you space, and tidies away the sort of clutter that can otherwise make a small room feel like a store cupboard.

Hanging arrangements Peg rails are neater than the traditional multi-purpose hall stand. If you don't want a whole row of coats making your hall feel even narrower than it is, you can

---

▶ *In a small home, you don't want to waste valuable living space, so a hall that has a practical purpose as well is extra-useful. This door opens directly into a little cloakroom, with a hanging rail that takes up minimal space for storing coats, and built-in cupboards to keep it all neat. Light, pinkish walls and woodwork ensure that it feels welcoming rather than functional. The washable floor tiles are pink terracotta, and the cupboard door panels have been highlighted in the same colour. To let in as much light as possible, the small window is left uncurtained, and the wide sill is used as a display shelf instead.*

◀ *Console tables that stand flush against the wall are a useful space-saving design.*

▶ *Floorboards laid in the more usual way – along the length the hall – will emphasize a corridor effect. But you can turn this to your advantage by hanging pictures to create an instant gallery. This will make the hall feel more welcoming and will also help to break up the wall space.*

opt for individual hooks positioned where they'll take up least room – a couple on either side of the door, for instance. If the hall is long and thin, it's a good idea to fix your coat rail flat against the far end so that it foreshortens the corridor effect as well as keeping it clear. Alternatively an old-fashioned hat stand will take up little space in a corner and, again, will keep coats out of the line of traffic. Gloves, torches, dog leads, hats and scarves all need to be stored where you can find them quickly on your way out and replace them neatly when you come in, so hooks and pegs are ideal.

Chests and blanket boxes A handy way of hiding wellingtons, bicycle pumps, torches and lots of other essential but unsightly paraphernalia neatly away. If your hall is wide enough to take something of this size, you'll also benefit from an extra table top for the telephone, directories, address books, visitors' book and so on.

Console tables A good solution where space is short. These are slim tables designed to stand flush against the wall. Console tables with a curved front are particulary useful for narrow rooms, as they take up less space both visually and practically than a square-cornered piece.

◀ *A light, neutral scheme for a hall that has been opened up to incorporate the bottom of the staircase as part of the space. Rubber flooring provides a washable surface in the main hall area, but the effect is softened by light wood planking for the stairs, cleverly extended to make a deep shelf-cum-seat for the telephone and so on. A plain Venetian blind lets in plenty of light.*

HALL DETAILS

Other items to put on your hall shopping list range from the strictly functional to the neatly practical.

Door furniture Numbers, name plates, door-knobs, knockers, bells, escutcheons (keyhole surround and cover) and letter boxes – all the practical details that keep you in touch with the outside world.

Notice board Somewhere to stick reminders, messages and shopping lists.

Key cabinet A slim, wall-mounted cupboard fitted with several rows of hooks to keep all your keys in one place.

Letter/pen tray The hall is a collecting point for mail, business cards, useful phone numbers and so on. A letter holder of some sort will keep it all tidy and can also hold pens and pencils for taking messages. (Cutlery trays are a useful size.)

Door curtain For extra insulation or to dress up a functional door.

▼ *A key cabinet will keep essential items where you know you can find them. You'll want pens handy for messages, and somewhere to keep mail and reminders tidy – a cutlery tray is useful for this.*

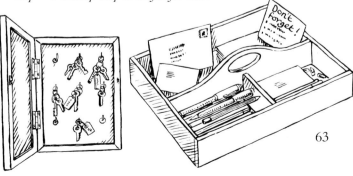

63

Living Rooms

All-purpose living rooms need to provide the best of all worlds. A room to relax, work, read and entertain in has a lot to live up to. This is the place that guests will see most of, especially if it's used as a dining room too. It's also the room whose furnishings are going to get most wear, and the one you'll tire of fastest if you make the wrong decorating decisions. So it's worth taking time to plan what you want.

The first job of a living room is to provide an easy, relaxing place to spend time, so don't plan anything too formal. You want to aim for something that looks good but is practical enough for everyday use – and your guests will be far more impressed with a room that feels really comfortable than with a scheme that's too smart to touch!

If you use the room as a work area, you'll need at least part of it to maintain an organized, clutter-free structure where you can keep books, papers and other work in order. If you have children, it may end up as a playroom too, in which case your choices will have to be hard-wearing, easy-to-clean and non-breakable. And as well as providing enough seating for however many people you envisage using the room at one time, it's going to need storage space for things like televisions, video recorders, hi-fi equipment, books, records, cassettes and CDs.

COLOUR AND STYLE

More than any other room, your living room will identify your own personal style. Because it's the room people will see most, it's the one they'll automatically associate with where you live. But if it's going to be all things to all people, it can't afford to be *too* unusual in style, so stick to a versatile colour scheme – and save your more idiosyncratic ideas for your own bedroom.

The first thing to bear in mind is that the living room will get more daytime use than most areas of your home, so when you're choosing the wall colour, think about the direction it faces and the amount of natural light available. You don't want a living room to be gloomy or mysterious, so look for a colour with a good light-reflective quality. This doesn't mean that you're stuck with white: soft blues, aquas and mauves will all work well in brightly lit sitting rooms (and will also help to cool the effect if it's *too* bright), while yellows and pinkish creams will warm up a darker room.

Once you've got a light, relaxing background to work against, you can add darker floor and furniture colours that won't show the signs of everyday use. You can then start adding your

▶ *A multi-purpose living room needs a place for everything. In this apartment it's been achieved with a clever storage unit that provides display and book shelves, hi-fi storage and neat floor cupboards. The jazzy patterned sofa is the focal point of the room – and the unifying factor too. It combines several shades of blues and greens which are then picked up in the wall colour, the woodwork detail, the plain sofa, the small dining table and the green accessories. Using two different sofa fabrics like this works very well; a second sofa in the patterned fabric would have been too much for a small room, but the two together balance each other perfectly.*

own personal style with accessories and details – painting woodwork in a contrasting colour, using your favourite colours for curtains and cushion covers, and hanging pictures to add interest to the walls.

If you can afford one major purchase for your new home, a good-looking sofa is a really worthwhile investment and will provide a starting point for your colour scheme. This has worked very well in the blue living room shown on page 65.

LIVING-ROOM LIGHTING

Your lighting needs to be at its most flexible in the living room, adapting from daytime to evening use and changing the mood from practical to restful. So plan your lights carefully, make sure that you've plenty of power sockets to provide lamps where you need them, and if possible fit dimmer switches so that the level is easy to adjust.

The bigger the room, the more difficult it is to light with a single overhead fitting, so living rooms really benefit from wall lights and side lamps. Floorstanding uplighters are particularly useful as they can be moved around to highlight different areas. For instance, if you're entertaining friends for dinner you can position your lights around the eating area so that the predominant feel is of a dining room; or if you just want to sit and relax you can readjust the lights so that the sofa and chairs are the focal point.

Task lighting in a sitting room doesn't need the strong beam of a kitchen work area. If you're using it for reading or sewing, it's the direction of the light that's more important. Jointed lamps

▶ *A cool, contemporary colour scheme for a room that mixes traditional and modern styles very effectively. Keeping the colours neutral is a good idea for a living room as it gives you the chance to add colour gradually as you collect more furniture and accessories – you can see how the odd splash of red here stops the beiges and creams from appearing drab or monotonous. Mixing different neutrals works well too, so despite the cream upholstery the room has a practical, everyday feel.*

such as the Anglepoise are ideal, but if you'd prefer something less functional-looking a well-positioned table lamp or floorstanding lamp will do the same job. Alternatively fix a rise-and-fall pendant light where you can lower it over a work table.

Don't forget firelight if you've got it. The flames of a real fire don't shed enough light to be of any practical use, but they add atmosphere and a sense of movement to a room, particularly if you have polished wood or glass for the light to reflect in.

For more ideas see chapter on Lighting.

LIVING-ROOM FLOORS

Living rooms tend to be redecorated and refurnished more frequently than other rooms in the house, so it's a good idea to stick to a fairly neutral floor that won't need changing every time you buy a new set of cushions. It's also one of the larger areas you're going to furnish, so you'll be limited by what you can afford.

Wood boards, a fitted natural floorcovering or a neutral-coloured fitted carpet are your easiest options – in ascending order of economy! Rugs can be laid on top to add colour and pattern, and if you *are* likely to change your decorations again, remember that wood can be painted too. A wood floor with a painted or stencilled border around the edge can give a similar effect to a traditional loose-laid carpet but at a fraction of the cost.

A natural floorcovering will have a much stronger sense of texture than carpet, so it's a good choice if your walls and furnishing fabrics are plain.

In warm climates, terracotta tiles are a good alternative to wood and will keep the room beautifully cool. Like wood, they're also a good background for loose rugs if you don't want a hard floor underfoot. The variety of terracotta shades – including very light-creamy pinks – is particularly useful in matching different furnishings.

For more ideas see chapter on Floors.

INSTANT LIVING-ROOM STYLES

Pretty and contemporary Light, pastel colours. Pinks and peaches with soft greens; blues and misty greys; aqua and lilac. White woodwork. Floors in muted natural or pastel colours, or wood with pretty rugs.

Minimal and understated White or cream walls. Wood or natural matting on the floor. Recessed ceiling lights, with wall washers and uplighters. Keep fabrics plain – linens and muslins – or choose simple black and white designs such as toile de jouy or striped mattress ticking. Make a display of black-and-white prints or photos in inexpensive frames.

Faded and traditional Tapestry-work fabrics. Velvet cushions – and the colours of faded velvet for other fabrics and carpets: deep rose, old gold, moss green. Traditional-style woven rugs. Wall bracket lights and painted-wood chandelier fittings.

Country cottage Shutters instead of curtains. Painted wood and wicker furniture. Small-patterned fabrics and prints – flower sprigs, checks, polka dots and ginghams. Plain cottons. Display shelves and plate racks.

Bright and tropical Blues, greens, lemon and violet. Vivid citrus and parrot colours. This is the sort of look that can almost turn a room into a conservatory. Light wood and cane furniture, or painted wood. Crisp cotton fabrics. Terracotta- and ceramic-tiled floors.

LIVING-ROOM FURNITURE
Planning the Shape

Keep the overall shape of the room in your mind as you position your furniture. This is important in any room, but particularly in a living room. Because the space has so many roles to play, it's all too easy to fill it with more and more useful items until it becomes a sort of shapeless muddle. The smaller the room, the more carefully you have to plan it.

Work out your sight lines while the room is more or less empty. Look at it from the doorway and from where you're planning to put your sofa or favourite chair: these are the two most frequent views you'll get of the room as a whole. Windows and fireplaces are natural focal points, and in rooms with good light there may be an area of interest opposite the window, where the light falls.

Seating

The traditional three-piece suite is far too big and cumbersome for most living rooms, because if you want a good-size sofa you get two hefty armchairs as well. If there's space for only one large piece of furniture, you're far better off splashing out on exactly the sofa you want and then adding smaller-scale chairs and stools. Low fabric-covered footstools or higher piano-stool designs can be kept out of the way beneath a table when not in use, and plain wooden stools will double as occasional tables too. And because they're not part of a set, their use is far more flexible – you can always move one of them on to a bedroom or wherever else it's needed.

Don't feel constrained to stick to the three-piece suite 'triangle' either. You probably won't have much choice about where you put the sofa, but think practically about where the other chairs will look best and be most help. Consider which areas of the room will get most use, and the places people will need to reach. And don't be tempted to arrange all the seating facing the television – it makes a very unattractive focal point!

Remember that if your sofa is a convertible sofa bed and will sometimes be used to put up overnight guests, it needs to be positioned where you can fold out the bed without having to move other furniture. Don't box it in between pieces that are too heavy to shift easily.

Another option is to do without a sofa altogether. A mix of chairs in different styles and fabrics looks just as good, and makes more use of the space. Or you can use a chaise-longue or day bed as an alternative sofa. The advantage of both these is that they haven't the usual padded back of the sofa, so they won't project as far into the room. The traditional chaise-longue has an arm rest on one side only – like half a sofa – which makes it much less bulky and doesn't cut across the room so obtrusively. A day bed, usually designed on a wooden frame curving up into low, carved arms at both sides, can be set flat against a wall and piled with cushions which will act as a back rest.

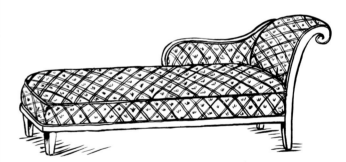

▲ *A chaise-longue may be a neater option than a sofa. Because it hasn't any arms it will look smaller and less cumbersome.*

▲ *A day bed can be stood flat against a wall, with cushions added to provide a comfortable back rest.*

Instant Upholstery

If you're stuck with a shabby second-hand chair or sofa, or one that doesn't match the room, you can improvize a quick new cover very effectively with lengths of attractive fabric. A rug or blanket can literally be thrown over a chair or sofa – just drape it over the back, or at an angle down across one arm. The essence of a fabric throw is that however carefully you've arranged it, it should look as though it's just been casually tossed into place!

Remember that cushions will go a long way towards disguising a sofa. With lots of cushions piled on the seat, only the back will be visible – and this can be neatly covered by a pretty rug.

If you want to hide the whole thing, you're better off using a length of lightweight inexpensive fabric. This can simply be tucked into place between cushions and chair arms to create a brand-new no-sew loose cover. Corners can be

▲ *Use a pretty rug to cover the back of the sofa and add lots of cushions for colour and comfort.*

▲ *For a complete cover-up, colourful bedspreads and lengths of sheeting fabric (very wide fabric designed for making bed linen) can be used to swathe the whole sofa.*

▲ *Shabby chair and sofa upholstery can be given an instant face lift with a rug or fabric throw. A length of bright fabric just draped over one arm will make all the difference. Fabric can also be draped over the back and seat and tied in a knot at the front.*

◄ *Gather the fabric at the front of each arm and pin it in place so that it falls into simple pleats – you can stitch on a button or a big bow as an extra trim.*

70

▲ *If the room has a natural alcove or recess, this is the easiest place to fit shelves. Make use of all the available space – right up to the ceiling.*

▲ *If your sitting room is pushed for space, remember that you can use the area above the door. This is empty space that's worth taking advantage of.*

discreetly pinned and disguised with bows or rosettes, and you can neaten the effect with buttons stitched along the back and on the fronts of the arms to keep the shape in place.

Display and Storage

If the room has an alcove or recess, this may be the most practical place to install a cupboard or set of shelves without taking up valuable floor space. You can opt for the cheapest slot-in metal strut and bracket system here, as the recess sides will make built-in shelf ends – and if the shelves are going to be fairly solidly lined with books, tapes and hi-fi equipment, these will also disguise the support brackets effectively.

Don't assume that filling a recess is your only option, though. If you like the shape the alcove gives the room, you may be better to leave it free and add a freestanding unit or wall cabinet elsewhere. In a small room, for example, an openwork design such as wrought iron or wirework will give a far slimmer impression than a solid bookcase or bureau.

Items such as clocks and vases can look good displayed on their own individual shelves. You can support a small shelf on a right-angled wall bracket. A variety of ready-made shelf supports

and brackets are available from DIY stores – from plain wood to pretty, lightweight, cast-aluminium brackets designed to look like old-fashioned architectural ironwork. And high-level shelves can provide both storage and display space overhead, even above doorways.

Make the most of dual-purpose items like chests and blanket boxes, which are the ideal height for an occasional table as well as providing storage space inside.

▲ *Items like clocks and large vases can be displayed on individual shelves supported by a bracket. Pretty brackets designed like old-fashioned architectural ironwork are available in practical lightweight aluminium ready-drilled with holes for screwing into the wall and attaching a shelf.*

71

Fitted Furniture

If you are very pushed for space, back-to-the-wall furniture that keeps the centre of the room free can be the most practical solution. Built-in units will provide a clutter-free home for the television and hi-fi equipment as well as books and music. And armchair seating in block-designed units can be assembled into as long or short a sofa as you need and will fit neatly around corners without wasting space. This style of furniture tends to suit modern homes best, but the beauty of its modular construction is that you can add extra units as you need them, so it is very versatile and adaptable.

LIVING-ROOM CHECKPOINTS
● Don't try to cram in too much furniture – be ruthless and consider where else in the house various pieces might be useful.

● Keep the background colour light and versatile, and add more interest with furnishings and accessories.

● Stick to a neutral floorcovering, or a painted one so that the colour can be changed to match later furniture additions.

● Make sure that lighting can be adjusted to suit different moods and activities.

● Make use of inexpensive fabric lengths for loose furniture throws and instant cover-ups.

▶ *Piles of cushions and sofa throws give this white-painted living room a very comfortable, informal feel. Built on at the back of the house, the room had no natural light, so glass panels were let into the door and deep windows knocked through on either side of it, making it more like a conservatory. The terracotta floor adds to this effect.*

Kitchens

The idea of the kitchen as the heart of the home dates back to the days when kitchens were power houses of service and industry and had a staff to run them! Fitted furniture and neat appliances mean they now have all sorts of other benefits to offer – and are much more fun to decorate.

Practicality should be uppermost in your kitchen planning. Even if you're not a keen cook, or want a rustic, unfitted look, you will still need unobstructed access to cooker, fridge, sink, work tops and storage. And the kitchen is usually the room that has to accommodate all the general paraphernalia for which there's no room elsewhere, from cleaning equipment to spare light bulbs and fuses. Colour and decoration will make it a pleasant place to work, but the most important thing is that it suits the way you live. This chapter tells you how to plan a new kitchen – and how to update an old one at a fraction of the cost!

BASIC PLANNING

If you're planning your kitchen from scratch, there's no substitute for an accurate floor plan on which you can mark existing fittings, furniture and immovable features such as windows and plumbing points. Draw it to scale and mark all the measurements clearly.

The basis of a practical kitchen layout is the arrangement described by kitchen designers as the 'work triangle' – the space between cooker, sink and fridge. Your kitchen plan should allow for clear access to all three. You should be able to turn quickly and easily from one to another without the risk of dropping a hot pan or spilling an ice-cube tray. It's an easier arrangement to achieve in some kitchens than in others: long, thin kitchens have a natural tendency to line up all the appliances in a row, and in very small kitchens you really won't have much choice about what fits where. But if you aim for the triangle – even an elongated one – you'll have a good basis for the rest of your kitchen.

Individual requirements will vary according to how frequently – and what sort of food – you cook. If you're a keen gourmet you'll appreciate a good, long run of work surface. If, on the other hand, most of your meals go straight from the fridge into the microwave and on to a plate, you can make do with considerably less work space.

Cooks are always divided about whether things should be stored away or near at hand on open shelves, but they all agree that order is important. Work out what you're going to need most often and keep it where you can get at it.

Kitchen Planning Notes

● Take each room measurement (for example, floor to ceiling, wall to wall) at several different points to check for any inconsistencies and unevenness.

● Remember to take account of all projections such as pipework and meter housings.

▶ *A kitchen that changed course half-way through – and proof that you can mix different styles very effectively. This kitchen was originally going to be fully fitted with wall cupboards that matched the base units, but once the base run had been installed, the owners decided that the small room couldn't cope with any more of the dark cupboard fronts, so they changed their plans and went for open shelves instead. The mix of high-tech black and red with light wood and cream tiles works very well because the two styles have been integrated so thoroughly – picking up the wood of the kickboard plinth to edge the tiled work top and to make the wall shelves.*

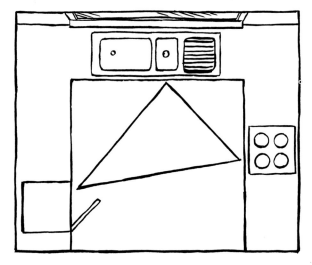

▲ *For the most practical working arrangement, the key elements of sink, cooker and fridge should form a triangle to enable easy access from one to another.*

● Mark the existing plumbing points on your plan – if you want to install a washing machine, for instance, you will need to run pipework to the sink wastepipe.

● Mark the position of existing power points: it's not usually difficult to add more, but you may as well make the best use of what's there.

● Work out which way you want cupboard and fridge doors to open for easiest access.

● Plan where you are going to need task lighting – this can be fixed discreetly under wall cabinets to illuminate work top areas.

● Don't site a hob or cooker top under a window where a draught might fan the flames of a gas ring, or curtains could be swept across the hob.

● Make sure that you leave a clear stretch of work top next to ovens and hobs as put-down space for hot pans and dishes.

● Don't plan for wall cupboards to be fitted above a hob.

● Don't site a fridge next to a cooker – it will have to work overtime to keep its cool.

● If you're replacing an existing kitchen, it's worth living with it for a while before you scrap it, to get an idea of exactly how you want to improve on it: where you'd prefer cupboards, and where drawers would be more practical; whether it's easier to stretch up or bend down to reach essential cooking items.

COLOUR AND STYLE

Kitchen styles fall into two main groups: streamlined and high-tech, to emphasize the room's status as a work centre; or softer and traditional, which makes it feel less functional and more lived-in.

The sleek, modern look provides simple lines and easy-to-clean surfaces, with no awkward corners. Kitchens in this style are good for small areas where too much decoration would feel cluttered and fussy; small kitchens really can't take a rustic, unfitted effect without looking a mess.

The more traditional styles tend to have wooden cabinets – you can go for anything from elegant mahogany-finish panelling to much plainer, planked-wood cupboard fronts for a more contemporary look. Styles like these are perfect for a larger room, especially if it's one you're going to spend a lot of time in. It's a softer, more furnished look that will create a comfortable background for meals round a kitchen table.

It's best to avoid the darker woods in a small kitchen, as they can seem rather gloomy and oppressive. Kitchens really benefit from light, practical colours that are refreshing to work in – which is why white units are so popular. If you want dark wood, try to include a couple of units with glass-fronted doors to lighten the effect, and open-shelf end units that will soften the corners.

However, there's so much variety in kitchen furniture nowadays that you can choose almost any style you like in any colour or finish. So if you're looking for a neat, white design, you're not limited to a clinical-finish melamine: you can just as easily find white-painted wood for a prettier, slightly country-style effect. Similarly, if you want the traditional lines of wood panelling, you can opt for a pretty painted colour (or paint it yourself!) rather than sticking to the natural wood-grain surface.

Kitchen Colours

Walls and ceilings should be kept light (there may not be much wall left to decorate if you've got a fitted kitchen). You can add pattern by using tiles for splashback areas immediately above sink and hob.

As mentioned in the chapter on Colour and Pattern, certain colours are traditionally associated with kitchen decoration. Blue and white are classic colours that have a distinctly country feel but are neat enough to work well in high-tech kitchens too. If you find blue too cold on its own, blue and yellow make a sunnier, summery combination.

Red and white will be cheerful and reassuringly practical, creating an instant feel of push-button simplicity. Subtler tones can be introduced by terracotta bread crocks or red quarry tiles on the floor to change the effect from functional city apartment to Mediterranean or farmhouse style.

FITTED OR FREESTANDING?

Whether to choose fitted or freestanding units largely depends on whether you want to hide everything away or keep it out on show. Fitted kitchens are the neatest way of making use of all the available space and have the advantage of providing a complete furnished look for the room in one go. But freestanding furniture like chests and dressers will add character and variety in a less functional style.

A good compromise, if you need the practicality of fitted units but want to give the room a more individual look, is to combine fitted and unfitted furniture. Use fitted units to make a neat work area around the sink and draining board, then add freestanding cupboards and chests where you want them. Or install fitted base units and work tops, but leave the wall space unfitted: open shelves and display units will give a lighter, more spacious effect.

INSTANT KITCHEN STYLES

Simple and contemporary White or plain wood cupboard fronts – with a few glazed doors too. Try mixing white and wood together: white units with a woodblock work top, or wooden base units with white-painted wall cupboards. Stripwood floor. Plain white roller blinds for the windows.

Sleek and high-tech Everything discreetly fitted, right up to the ceiling – no open storage except for ultra-functional chrome utensils on hanging rails. Recessed lighting. Granite-effect work tops. Black-and-white tiled floors. Slatted window blinds.

Bright and practical White cupboards with handles and trims in bold primary colours. Bright plastic utensils and stacking plastic storage containers. Chequered vinyl floor tiles. Simple curtains or roller blinds in bright colours.

Country style Light wood or painted cupboards with panel detailing. A few free-standing pieces of furniture if there's room. Open wall shelves and plate racks. Pretty china out on display. Blue-and-white or green-and-cream ceramic tiles. Traditional terracotta- or quarry-tiled floor.

Fitted Furniture

There's a unit for every purpose and every shape of room these days, so a fitted kitchen lets you organize the room exactly as you want.

Base units can be fitted with either cupboards or drawers. Many professional cooks consider drawers easier because you get an instant and

77

well-lit bird's-eye view of their contents instead of having to rummage around in the depths of a dark cupboard. Plinth drawers – shallow drawers fitted behind the unit kickboards at floor level – are a marvellous way of using otherwise wasted space, and some built-in oven-housing units are designed with a deep pan drawer in the base.

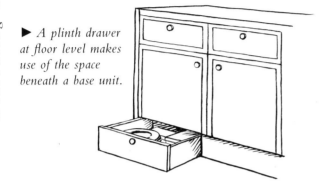

▶ *A plinth drawer at floor level makes use of the space beneath a base unit.*

Wall cupboards usually offer more variety of size than base units. Generally designed to sit much slimmer against the wall, they protrude around 300 mm (12 in) as opposed to 500 mm (20 in) or 600 mm (24 in) for base units. Where floor space is short, a run of base units in this slimmer size is a great help too – standard units can be cut to size by trimming a few inches off the back.

Wall units are available in different heights too, to fit different heights of ceiling. You can either run them right up to the ceiling to give you as much cupboard space as possible, or opt for shorter units and use the space on top to stand items like jugs and vases which you don't want to hide away.

All fitted kitchen units are available with a choice of right- or left-opening doors, so work out the arrangement which suits your kitchen layout best. Awkward corners can be dealt with by specially designed corner units to avoid any waste of space due to inaccessibility. Look for units with hinged doors which fold right back to give a clear view of the cupboard contents, and carousel fittings which can be swung out to expose the items stored furthest inside.

▲ *Two different ways to make the most of corner space. A double-hinged door will fold right back to give clear access to the cupboard. Carousel shelves that swing out with the door are a good way of getting at smaller items stored at the back.*

Make the most of all the space-saving and practical gadgets that fitted units can provide. Even if your kitchen isn't short of space, they are a marvellous way of tidying away essentials and keeping everything to hand for when you need it. Tall end-of-run cupboards can store cumbersome items such as mops and brooms. Hidden waste bins, chopping boards, extra pull-out work surfaces, wine racks and even ironing boards can all be incorporated. And you can have functional appliances such as fridges streamlined into the plan too, neatly hidden away behind matching door panels – especially useful if your kitchen is visible from an adjoining room.

▲ *Removable wire baskets for vegetables and cleaning equipment can be slotted on to runners so that they work like drawers.*

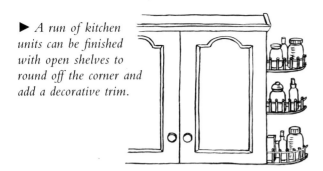

▶ *A run of kitchen units can be finished with open shelves to round off the corner and add a decorative trim.*

Freestanding Furniture

If you're happy to have much of your kitchen equipment on view, there are all sorts of open-storage options available. A row of butcher's hooks on a wall rail can be used to hang utensils above a work top so that they're near at hand. Old-fashioned ceiling-hung airers make good use of overhead space: these are excellent for pans, utensils and strings of vegetables. A curtain pole or length of dowelling can be fixed as a wall rack to do the same job, and peg rails can be used to hang mugs and utensils.

Butcher's trolleys are a godsend in both fitted and unfitted kitchens. Based on the traditional high-standing butcher's block, these are fitted with castors and with extra shelving and storage beneath the chopping board to provide a complete portable work station that can be wheeled into service whenever it's needed.

▲ *Hanging storage is useful for pans and utensils when cupboard space is tight.*

▶ *A butcher's trolley provides an extra work station wherever you need it. Topped with a chopping block, it can also house drawers, shelves, vegetable baskets and towel rails.*

DIY KITCHEN UPDATE

If you can't afford completely new kitchen cabinets, a quick face lift of the old ones will provide a custom-designed finish and is fun to do. The easiest way to transform old kitchen units is to paint them.

DESIGNING A DIY PAINTED KITCHEN

This technique will work for both melamine and wood units. First rub the surface down well with fine-gauge sandpaper to give it a good 'key' that will take the paint. Sponge down with warm water and a little detergent. When the surface is dry, apply an undercoat, then paint with oil-based paint – eggshell for a lower-sheen finish, or gloss. Either of these will provide a practical, washable finish for kitchen furniture. Decoration can be added by outlining the shape or adding an interesting paint finish, or by drilling a simple pattern.

On panelled wood units   The panelling provides natural lines that can be highlighted with a contrasting colour. Keep your brush fairly dry, working lightly over the moulding to build up the colour gradually. You can always add more as you get the hang of it.

On flush-fronted units   You can add fake panelling with lengths of beading or ready-made panels from timber merchants. Fix these before you paint the units – use a pencil to   79

mark the positions, stick them on with a good wood glue and then paint over the whole thing so that any pencil guidelines are covered up. Alternatively, you can paint your own *trompe l'oeil* panels. For this method you should paint the background colour first, and then mark on the outline of a panelled shape (measure up a panelled door of the same size to see how big the panels should be). For the most realistic effect, draw your fake panel as two outlines, each about 1 cm (½ in) wide, one inside the other. Paint the outer border in a slightly darker shade than the inner: this will give the effect of traditional moulding. Work out your colours on a piece of scrap wood before you start – you could even paint the centre of the panel a completely different colour from the main door.

Finishing   If you want a less solid finish, you can give the units a colourwashed effect by painting a second, thinner colour over the first. Again, experiment on a piece of scrap wood first, thinning down the second colour with turps or white spirit and brushing lightly to leave a streaky, slightly translucent finish. Brush in the direction of the grain, and following the shape of any panelling.

To protect your paintwork from splashes and wear, it's a good idea to finish the whole thing with a few coats of polyurethane varnish.

Drilling a pattern   This gives a very effective finish. Stick to an easy design such as a square or a diamond and practise on a piece of spare wood to get the hang of it. Work out the pattern carefully so that you've got exact guide marks for the holes to drill.

◀ *This kitchen manages to combine a pretty, country look with neatly fitted units that make the most of every available centimetre of space. The pale, sunny colour is the key element in making it feel so open and light, but to increase this effect, the door was removed as well. This meant that the doorway space could be used for extra cupboards on the left, and an additional shelf on the passage wall provides handy storage for small items.*

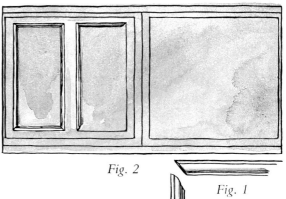

Fig. 2

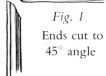

Fig. 1
Ends cut to
45° angle

▲ *Convert flush doors into panelled ones by sticking on wood moulding. The ends of each piece will need to be cut at a 45-degree angle to make the corners (Fig. 1). Stick the panel pieces in place with a good wood glue, easing them into position so that the corners make a neat fit (Fig. 2). Any imperfections can be filled with a blob of wood filler and then smoothed down: these will be hidden when you paint over the top.*

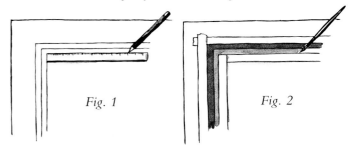

Fig. 1   *Fig. 2*

▲ *To paint a fake door panel, paint the background colour first. When it is completely dry, use a ruler and pencil to draw the panel as a double outline (Fig. 1). Then paint in your two borders with a fine paintbrush, using masking tape to help you get a sharply defined edge (Fig. 2).*

Work Tops
Work tops are functional, but they present an expanse of surface to full view, so you also want something that looks good and matches your colour scheme. If you do a lot of food preparation, think about incorporating a built-in chopping block as part of the work top.

Vinyl   The most basic and inexpensive finish. Laminated on a solid wood backing, it comes in a variety of colours and effects and can be finished with a wood or tile trim to give a neat edge. Patterned surfaces such as a marbled or speckled

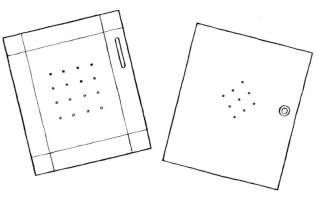

▲ *Plain cabinet doors can be decorated with a simple pattern of drilled holes.*

effect are more practical than a plain colour, as stains and scratches will show up less.

Woodblock More expensive but gives a wonderfully rich, mellow effect. (Don't be tempted to treat it as an extended chopping board or you'll quickly destroy the surface!)

Ceramic tiles Can be used to cover a whole run of work surface, bordered by a wood or tile trim. The grouting needs to be thorough, though, and is liable to stain easily, so you're better using larger tiles which need proportionately less grouting.

Marble The most expensive surface, traditionally used for pastry making because it stays so cool. If you're planning an unfitted kitchen, you may be able to incorporate a slab of marble supported on a cupboard or chest – or, even better, an old washstand with a ready–made marble top.

▶ *A collection of blue-and-white china was the starting point for this little kitchen, built into the corner of a one-room studio apartment. Keeping things out on show here was important to make it feel an integral part of the living area, so it was designed with plenty of open storage. A tall shelf unit effectively divides the kitchen from the rest of the room, and also ensures that the most frequently used china is easily accessible from both sides. The top of the wall units is used for extra display, and a shelf has been extended across the top of the window too. Hanging storage makes the most of the vertical space.*

Sinks and Taps

Essentials like sinks and taps are such an integral part of the kitchen that it's easy to forget what a variety there is to choose from.

Old-fashioned porcelain butler's sinks (the deep rectangular tanks that have been turned into so many container gardens over the years!) are still very appealing for country-style kitchens. The disadvantage with traditional installations was that the join between sink and adjacent wooden draining board was difficult to seal, allowing water and waste to get into the gap. If you're buying a new butler's sink, look for a design with an edge that overlaps the worktop, to avoid this problem.

Big sinks like these aren't really practical in small kitchens, though, and they don't offer many of the useful features of smaller, neater designs. A double sink is the best idea, so that you've one sink free for washing up if you're using the other for preparing food or draining pans. If you haven't room for two full-size sinks, a single sink with a half-size drainer will do the same job.

The most practical kitchen tap is a mixer that provides hot and cold water from one spout and can be swivelled if it needs to serve more than one sink. Look for lever handles too – these are easier to use than screw-top taps if your hands are wet or sticky from cooking.

▲ *The most practical sinks have a drainer bowl as well as the main sink. If you're short of work-top space, look for sinks with an integral chopping board that can be fitted over the sink or into the draining board.*

KITCHEN LIGHTING

Kitchen lighting is essentially functional, so it needs to be bright and well directed. Ceiling spots and downlighters will provide good general illumination, although if the ceiling is very high you may prefer a rise-and-fall pendant lamp which can be pulled into position over a table or work top.

More specific task lighting can be supplied by fluorescent strips fixed under wall units.

For more ideas see chapter on Lighting.

KITCHEN FLOORS

The most important consideration for a kitchen floor is that it's easy to clean. It also needs to be hard-wearing, but comfortable to stand on.

If you're laying a new floor, vinyl and linoleum are the most economical option and give you the widest choice of colours and patterns to match the rest of the room. Cork tiles are another practical and economical alternative and provide a warm, neutral background similar to wood or terracotta, but they will need sealing.

Ceramic tiles fit the first part of the bill and always look good, but they will be chilly underfoot in cold weather and they're not for the clumsy. Anything breakable will have little chance of surviving if dropped.

If you prefer the traditional look of wood, old boards can be painted with a washable finish, or varnished stripwood flooring laid to give a cleaner, more contemporary feel. And if your kitchen is used as a living area too, sisal and coir are a good way of achieving a warmer effect.

For more ideas see chapter on Floors.

KITCHEN WINDOWS

Blinds are more practical than curtains in a kitchen: you don't want flapping fabric getting in the way of your cooking or washing up. If you prefer curtains, one option is a purely decorative curtain that is never drawn across but hangs to one side (away from the hob) and is firmly held in place by a tie-back.

Shutters painted in an eggshell or gloss finish are even more practical because they can be

▼ *Where you don't have room for a full-size cupboard, built-in storage slots for wine bottles and trays will ensure that the space isn't wasted.*

▲ *A plate rack fixed above a sink will do double duty as a drainer and a storage shelf.*

wiped down to get rid of cooking smells and splashes. The neatest arrangement is to fit them with the panels hinged Z-wise, so that they can be pulled aside with a compact, concertina action.

For more ideas see chapter on Windows.

KITCHEN DETAILS

Accessories in a kitchen are never purely decorative, but the best of them look good as well as serving a practical purpose.

Storage jars Pretty containers will add extra colour and decoration. Even clear glass jars (useful for seeing instantly what's in them) will make your shelves as colourful as a sweet shop once they're filled with lentils and dried fruit.

Plate racks Technically designed for draining your washing up, these are also a marvellous way of keeping pretty china on show.

Cup hooks Hanging a whole row of cups or mugs along a shelf edge or wall will provide pattern and colour like an instant dado rail.

Utensil storage Keep essential tools where you can get at them easily. Gadgets can be hung on a rack or pole or stood in jars and jugs on the work top. Knife blocks keep handles within easy reach and blades safely out of the way.

Wine racks Can be built into a fitted kitchen, or freestanding on the floor or work top.

Linens Tea towels and table cloths can add as much colour as your curtain fabric. Fabric offcuts (you can even use dusters and tea towels here) made up into drawstring bags will keep things like pegs and laundry and shoe cleaning items neatly hung on a wall or door.

Knobs and handles Will make all the difference to the overall look, but think about the design you will find most practical too. D-shape handles may be easier to use with wet or sticky hands.

KITCHEN CHECKPOINTS

● Make sure that cooker, sink and fridge form a practical work triangle (see 'Kitchen Planning Notes', page 74).

● Don't waste time and effort trying to accommodate fittings you don't really need – concentrate on making the best use of the space for the way you want to use it.

● Organize your storage so that regularly used items are easy to reach.

● Make the most of wall space, ceiling hangers and wasted corners for extra storage.

● Ensure that the floor is hard-wearing and washable.

● Use portable trolleys and fold-away table tops to provide extra work surface.

Dining Rooms

With our homes becoming increasingly compact, fully fledged dining rooms are something of an endangered species nowadays. If you're lucky enough to have one, make the most of it. If you're not, there are plenty of ways to create alternative eating areas with both comfort and style.

The key elements in a dining room are something to sit on and a surface to eat off. You'll also need storage space for china, glasses, cutlery and table linen. And you'll want the setting to be practical for day-to-day use as well as providing a comfortable place to entertain.

COLOUR AND STYLE

If your home is large enough for you to allocate one room as a separate dining room, you'll have much more freedom in how you can decorate it. But in dining areas that belong to a kitchen or sitting room, you'll have to devise a scheme that fits in with the rest of the room. Either way, make sure that it matches your favourite china!

The dining room is one place that can actually benefit from feeling enclosed, so don't worry if you haven't much space to play with. A small dining room can work just as well in warm, rich colours as in the lighter shades more usually chosen for a small room.

The table provides a natural centre and focuses attention into the room rather than towards the edges, and deeper colours will help make the place feel more cosy and reassuring, especially for winter or evening meals. Walls painted in rich terracottas and deep greens are good colours for this sort of look.

If you find this look too claustrophobic – or if you want to make the most of a dining room that overlooks a garden – you can use lighter colours to open up the space. Pastel walls and fabrics work well with pale woods and cane and provide a restful setting at any time of day. Or you can go for a cooler effect altogether by avoiding traditional wood furniture. A glass-topped table will look much less obtrusive, and will reflect your lighting well at night. Marble is another alternative surface – it's not so reflective, but it can be used to introduce other soft colours such as blues, greys and pinks. A small marble café-style table

▶ *A small and rather shabby room has been revamped with clever paint and fabric effects at very little expense. The one big advantage of the room is that it gets good natural sunlight, so glowing, sunny colours were used to make the most of this and open up the space. The other dominant feature is the impressive marble fireplace, and this inspired the dramatic decorative theme. The table itself is basic plywood, but dressed with a full-length cloth and trimmed to match the curtains it looks fit for any occasion. The chairs were a set, but rather battered, so the best solution for these was to give them a new coat of paint: they were finished with a sponged effect so that the odd dent and scratch is cleverly disguised. The walls have also been sponged – in yellow on white. This gives a light, translucent effect that reflects the sunlight, and also softens the wall area so that it looks less obtrusive than a flat colour: very useful in a small room. Finally, because the ceiling was quite high for the size of the room, making it feel tall and thin, another length of yellow fabric was used to create an opulent tented effect, lowering the ceiling and transforming it into a much warmer, cosier place to eat.*

won't break the bank and is a good solution for small eating areas.

If your dining area is part of a sitting room or kitchen, it's important that it looks equally good by day and at night. For rooms like this light walls will be the most versatile background, as something too dark and rich may feel gloomy in daytime, but you want to add colour in fabric and accessories so that the effect isn't too pristine and can stand up to everyday use. You can use different colours to adapt the mood of the room for different times of day. For instance, a soft yellow background can be matched with cushions and table linen in a fresh, practical blue during the day and dressed up with deep greens and golds for a special evening occasion.

ROOM DIVIDERS

When your dining area is part of another room, you want to make it feel distinct and contained but without creating a decorative clash with the rest of the room. There are two routes you can follow: either creating a physical barrier that divides the two areas, or suggesting a boundary line by a change in decorative style.

Creating a Partition

One of the simplest ways of demarcating your boundary is by positioning furniture so that it creates a natural dividing line. A dining room that is part of a kitchen can be separated from it by a run of kitchen units part-way across the room. These can be made doubly practical if you fit the 'backs' of the units with a second set of doors instead of rigid panels, so that the cupboards are accessible from the dining area as well. In a sitting room, a similar effect can be achieved with a chest or sofa positioned at right angles.

A full-length curtain hung on a pole at ceiling height will create an alternative screen and is more flexible as a part-time measure (see the curtained-off dining room on page 88. It can be drawn back against the wall when not in use, and tied with a cord or gathered into a tie-back.

Another option, if you want to be able to keep the space as one large area when the dining room is not being used, is a floorstanding screen. A basic screen can be made from hinged panels of wood painted or covered with fabric or paper.

MAKING A WOODEN SCREEN

■ You'll need a minimum of three panels for the screen to stand firmly. Cut them out of 1-cm ($\frac{1}{2}$-in) medium density fibreboard or plywood (plywood is lighter, but has a rougher, more absorbent surface which is more time-consuming to paint). The tops can be cut straight across, or shaped into arches or points.
■ Decorate the panels before fixing them together. The simplest way is to paint them. You can choose a plain colour to match your woodwork or furnishings, or add a border in a different colour. Alternatively decorate the panels with pasted-on paper motifs (see 'Decorating with Découpage', page 118).
■ For a more dressy finish, you can cover the screen with fabric or wallpaper. Cut the material slightly larger than the panel so that it can be folded over around the edges. Stretch it over the panel (you'll need to make small cuts into this border at corners and around curves so that it folds flat) and use a staple gun to fix it in place along the sides. If you want a

◀ *If your eating area is part of another room, hanging a curtain is the best way of making a temporary partition. This curtain effectively creates a separate room altogether. Made from two different fabrics, it matches the floral sitting-room upholstery on one side and has a gingham backing on the other – more in keeping with the practical stripes of the dining-room chairs. Gingham tabs are used to tie the curtain on to a wooden pole, so it's easy to remove if you want to use the room as a single area again. (And you can see from this combination how well the unexpected mix of florals and checks works if you stick to a consistent colour theme.) In the dining area itself, the painted kitchen plate rack provides a practical way of storing china without taking up much room.*

double-sided screen, cover the reverse side in the same way. Cover the raw edges with a length of braid or ribbon around each panel.

■ Each panel will need two sets of hinges – top and bottom – to join it to the next. The simplest way is to hinge pairs of panels alternately front and back, but make sure that you keep right sides matching if your screen is decorated only on one side. Lay the first two panels face down, aligning them carefully top

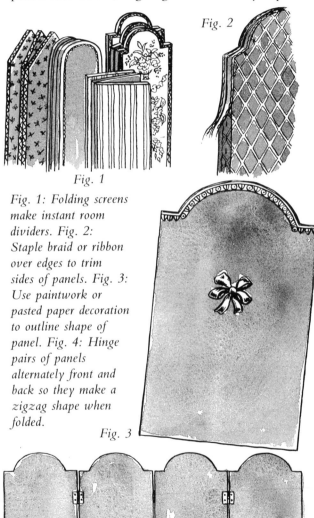

Fig. 2

Fig. 1

Fig. 1: Folding screens make instant room dividers. Fig. 2: Staple braid or ribbon over edges to trim sides of panels. Fig. 3: Use paintwork or pasted paper decoration to outline shape of panel. Fig. 4: Hinge pairs of panels alternately front and back so they make a zigzag shape when folded.

Fig. 3

Fig. 4

and bottom and keeping the sides parallel, and position the hinges so that they link the two panels. Screw them into place, then turn the pair of panels so that the right side is uppermost and the hinges are hidden underneath. Now attach the next panel, checking that it faces the same way as the others. This time the hinge will be on the front, so when the screen is folded it forms a zigzag shape.

Defining with Decoration

Using the decor to define the dining area is a better option if the room is too small to feel comfortable with a partition and you want to maintain a sense of space. Painting the walls a different colour in this part of the room, or using a different wallpaper, will instantly suggest a change of scene.

A change of flooring will have the same effect. For example, if the sitting room is carpeted, you could leave the dining area with plain or painted wooden boards. Or to demarcate the dining part of a tiled-floor kitchen, put down an area of sisal or seagrass, which will preserve the serviceable feel but add a hint of comfort.

DINING-ROOM LIGHTING

Mood is the most important effect to establish in a dining room. You won't need task lighting unless the room is to be used as a study or work area too.

Most overhead fittings will give too harsh a glare, killing the look of your food and table setting as well as making people sitting around it feel uncomfortable, but a rise-and-fall pendant is a practical compromise – this can be pulled down to illuminate the table effectively without dazzling people's eyes.

For parties and entertaining, side lamps and uplighters will add enough soft background light for people to eat and talk by, and candlelight is invaluable for atmosphere. Ceiling-hung candelabra suspended just above the table will provide atmospheric candlelight without taking up valuable table space.

For more ideas see chapter on Lighting.

INSTANT DINING-ROOM STYLES

Warm and cosy Rich, bold colours mixed with warm wood surfaces. Candlelight and brass. Tartan fabrics and comfortable leather furniture. Wooden shutters at the window.

Rich and formal Dark polished wood, deep colours. Crisp white table linen. Glass-fronted cabinets. Lots of reflective surfaces – perfect for rooms with an open fire. Heavy curtain fabrics. Candlestick lamps and candelabra.

Light and elegant Pastel colours, pinks and greens if it's a garden room, soft impressionist floral fabrics. Pale woods, possibly colourwashed. Glass candlesticks.

Bistro or conservatory style Cane furniture or light wood (or a glass- or marble-topped table). Lots of plants. Plain white blinds or bright jungle-print curtains in greens and blues.

Informal and cottagey Pine furniture or painted wood. China displayed on dressers and plate racks, checked table linen and crisp cotton curtains in checks or stripes.

DINING-ROOM FLOORS

The floor you choose will obviously depend on the style of the room as a whole, but some options are more practical than others.

Carpet will give the room a warm, comfortable feel, but you may find that chair legs leave dents and wear marks from being constantly sat on and shifted. A patterned design will show these less, or you could lay a central patterned rug over a plain background colour.

Traditional dining rooms – especially in a more formal style – always look smart with a wood floor, but boards will be subject to scratches and dents from chair legs, so again an additional rug is a good idea. If the boards aren't in the best of condition, painting them will cover up stains and repairs – this has worked very well in the yellow dining room shown on page 87. For dining rooms decorated in a conservatory style, or that lead straight out to a garden, there's nothing to beat traditional tiles. If you're laying a patio outside, you could consider budgeting for an extra set of terracotta tiles to continue the effect indoors. But if the cost is prohibitive, you can create your own 'tiled' floor very effectively by painting it (see page 43 for how to paint a chequered floor).

DINING-ROOM FURNITURE
Tables

The sort of table you choose will depend on how much room you have and how many people you want to be able to seat. Always be careful to measure the height of the table top, especially the distance from the underside to the floor (this is where it will matter to people's knees!). Some old-fashioned kitchen tables – particularly those with a built-in cutlery drawer – don't give you enough clearance for chairs to fit underneath comfortably.

If space is at a premium in your dining room, a circular table will take up less of it. Some circular tables are designed with a surface that can tilt upright so that the whole thing stores flat against a wall.

Gate-legs or drop-leafs (usually oblong, sometimes circular or oval) also fold away, in two side panels, the central panel giving you a narrow table surface when it's not in use. Extra storage is always useful, so look for cutlery drawers and cupboards – these are sometimes built into the side of a gate-leg table.

If you never need to seat more than two or three people, you might be best off with a small, circular table that will sit neatly in the corner of a kitchen or sitting room. A café-style marble-top

91

table on a cast-iron base will look good holding plants or photos when it's not being used as a dining table.

Seating

Dining-room chairs need to be comfortable and reliable – you have to be an extremely good cook for people not to notice that their backs are getting stiff or their knees keep bashing the table leg! Delicate rush-woven seats won't stand up to the sort of constant use chairs will get here: any chairs that you treasure for their decorative value are best kept well out of sight.

The most comfortable dining chairs have a rigid back and a cushioned seat. Traditionally a set of plain upright chairs comes with two carvers – of the same design but with carved wooden arms. Carvers look wonderful but remember that they will take up more room, because the arms prevent them from being pushed back under the table when they're not in use.

Chairs with cushioned seats give you a chance to add more colour and pattern to the room. Drop-in seats can be re-covered quite simply when you want to change the look, or if you've a

▼ *Drop-in chair seats are easy to re-cover if you want to match curtains or other upholstery. Push the seat out from below and remove the old cover. Add more padding if the cushion is starting to feel thin and flat, and cut a panel of new fabric to fit it – enough to fold around the seat edges so that you can tack it in place underneath.*

second-hand set you'd like to revamp. Upholstered seats require more work and expense, but you could refurbish them with flat tie-on cushions instead.

Tie-on cushions will also make kitchen or hard-back chairs comfortable enough to use at the dining table. Old chairs that are in sound condition but looking a little the worse for wear can be transformed with a couple of coats of paint. And you can turn a collection of junk-shop finds or hand-me-downs into a completely matching or co-ordinating set by dressing them in fabric covers (see page 94).

Much more slimline are plain wooden benches which will line up refectory-style on either side of a rectangular table. They can also be used as side tables against a wall when not needed for seating, or slotted out of sight altogether beneath the table. Benches let you squeeze more people around the table if you've invited friends for supper, and they're unbeatable for children's parties.

When space is really tight – or if you want to transform a study into a dining room in seconds – folding chairs are a godsend. The classic director's chair (canvas stretched over a collapsible wooden frame) still looks good, and you can always change the fabric covers when they get worn or outdated. Plain slatted designs (like old-fashioned church-hall chairs) are more practical for a dining table, and can be folded away flat or even hung on a wall hook for storage.

Disguising Old and Mismatched Wood

If you're stuck with odd chairs and a table that don't match (family cast-offs and junk-shop finds, for instance), you can turn them into a set quite easily.

A mixture of plain and painted woods looks effective – try painting the chairs and leaving the table its natural colour, or paint the table legs and the chairs and leave the table top plain. For an all-over opaque finish, you'll need to prime the wood first and then add a couple of coats of emulsion or eggshell paint.

A 'distressed' finish is even quicker to achieve,

92

▶ *One corner of a sitting room has been redecorated to make this little dining area. A round table on a single central pedestal is a neat idea wherever you're short of space – this one is pretty enough not to need covering with a cloth, and will also provide an effective display surface when the room isn't being used for eating. Old hard-backed chairs have been turned into something much more comfortable by the addition of cushioned seats, and the frilled skirts have the dual purpose of covering up signs of wear and co-ordinating with the sitting-room upholstery. The fitted sitting-room wall furniture also maintains a unifying theme: this end of the storage units has been commandeered to create a dresser effect, and provides cupboard space for china and cutlery.*

as your paintwork doesn't need to be perfect. You'll get the best effect if you use two slightly different colours of water-based emulsion. For a bleached, driftwood look, paint the lighter colour on first, leave it to dry and then add the darker shade, brushing quite lightly so that the undercoat shows through in streaks. Your chairs may not look any newer than they did, but at least you'll have a matching set!

For a less permanent option, both chairs and tables can be dressed with pretty fabric and changed as often as you want.

TO MAKE A DROP-OVER CHAIR COVER

■ For an upright chair, this is the easiest sort of cover to make as it simply involves cutting panels to fit each of the chair's surfaces. Take all the measurements carefully: the width of the seat and the distance from the back of the chair legs to the front of the seat; from the top of the back to the top of the seat; from the top of the back to the floor; and from the top of the seat to the floor.
■ Add an extra 2.5 cm (1 in) to each measurement to make sure that the cover isn't too tight a fit, and another 2 cm (1 in) to allow for seams and turnings, then cut fabric lengths to fit. Cut the back of the cover (top of seat back

to floor) as one panel. The front panel will cover the front of the chair back *and* the seat itself *and* the drop to the floor. You can either cut these as separate pieces, to make the most of your fabric width (in which case you'll need to add extra seam allowances to each piece) or you can add the three measurements together and cut them as one panel. Finally cut the two side panels that will cover the space between front and back legs.
■ If you're making the front from three pieces, stitch these together first, right sides facing. Then attach the front to the back along the top join. Hang your cover over the chair back inside out, pushing the front panel into place over the seat. Now pin the seat-to-floor side panels to fit. When you're happy with the way the cover sits, stitch the side panels in place along the sides of the seat and down the front legs. Turn the raw edges down front and

93

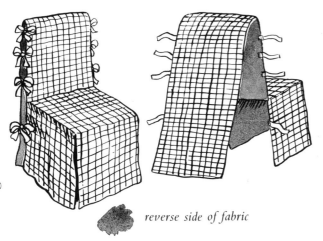

reverse side of fabric

▲ *Making a drop-over fabric cover for an upright chair is simply a matter of stitching together panels of fabric to fit seat, back and the distance to the floor. Attach ribbons or small fabric strips to the open sides so that you can tie the cover in place.*

back panels and attach ribbons or fabric strips to tie them together. Turn right-side out and hem the bottom of the skirt to the length you want.

Storage and Display

Old-fashioned dining rooms were always equipped with a sideboard, a vast all-purpose piece of furniture designed with drawers, cupboards and shelves to house all the accoutrements of the dining table from cutlery to condiments. Dressers fulfil the same function in a less formal, more kitchen-style way, being less concerned with hiding everything away and instead making more of a display of it.

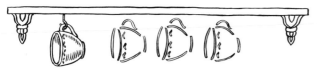

▲ *Design yourself a whole set of matching cups hanging from hooks. With a basic stencil pattern you can copy a favourite cup or mug and repeat it as many times as you like along a narrow shelf. See page 117 for how to cut a stencil motif.*

Few dining rooms have space for either of these nowadays, but you can create your own dresser effect by fixing wall shelves above a floorstanding chest or cupboard. The best shelves for a dining room are designed with a groove or slot in each one so that plates can be stood upright without slipping. Some also have a front bar to hold cups in place, or a row of hooks fixed along the lower edge to let you hang mugs and cups by their handles, which takes up less space.

Make the most of the existing shelf space offered by mantelpieces, window sills and display rails above window pelmets. In a kitchen dining area, a wall-hung or work-top plate rack can do double duty as a drainer and a storage unit, keeping plates on display and easy to reach.

If you want to store tableware safely away from the risk of breakages, glass-fronted cabinets keep pretty china on view but behind doors. In a small room, a corner unit will take up less space and also keep the cabinet neatly out of the way where it won't be at risk from kicks or collisions if there are children about. Some are sensibly designed in two parts, with a plain cupboard door in the lower half and the glass door higher up out of easy reach.

But there's no need to feel you have to stick to furniture designed solely for dining-room use. The secret is to think laterally. A bathroom washstand is a slim-fitting alternative to a sideboard, and many will have a drawer which will take a cutlery tray. Or a plain-fronted wardrobe – as long as it's fitted with shelves, not hanging rails – will make an ideal larder cupboard. You can use the bottom shelf as a drinks cabinet and the upper levels for table linen, glasses and so on.

Some of the best dining-room furniture is portable and can be kept out of the way when not in use. Trolleys can be wheeled into service when an extra side table is needed. And old-fashioned high-sided butler's trays are designed to fit on to a stand so that they can change from tray to table in an instant. The best of them also have sides which fold down to form a completely flat surface, and the whole thing – frame and tray together – folds neatly away for storage.

DINING-ROOM WINDOWS

Unless your dining room has a particularly good view, you may want to screen at least the lower half of the window. Eating – even a celebratory meal – isn't necessarily something you want to do in full public view. Slatted blinds, lace or muslin panels and half-length café curtains will all preserve privacy for daytime eating without blocking any light.

If you want to make a feature of the window, you can co-ordinate the room by matching curtain fabric to your table linen. But dining rooms don't really need a focal point other than the table, so a plain roman or roller blind will be just as effective, and shutters will do the same job without framing the window so obviously.

DINING-ROOM DETAILS

Table linen Traditional white cotton and damask always look good for table cloths and napkins, or you can opt for a fabric that adds colour and pattern to the room, or that matches curtains and upholstery. Plasticized fabric that can be wiped clean now comes in all sorts of designs from checks to leopard skin.

Napkin rings These keep individual napkins tidy at each place setting – from plain brass or silver rings to bright-coloured or intricately worked ornaments that add decoration to table tops in their own right. You can improvize a ring by tying the napkin with a pretty ribbon or cord.

Place mats and coasters Traditionally cork-based or woven rush, also available in more modern patterned acrylic designs, to prevent hot plates and cups from damaging the table. Padded fabric to match napkins or curtains will do the same job. Or improvize with decorative ceramic tiles – you'll need to lay a cloth first, or back them with a felt base, to make sure that they won't scratch the surface.

Candlesticks and candelabra These add instant atmosphere even if you retain background lighting too. Can be decorated with greenery and flowers wound around the base. If you're worried about wax dripping on to the table, a glass-shaded hurricane lamp is a good alternative, and also reflects the candlelight very effectively.

Baskets For bread, fruit and so on. Line with a crisp napkin or tea towel – or use a plain basket to hold a neat pile of napkins instead of distributing them with individual rings.

Decanters and water jugs Anything from cut crystal to an earthenware pitcher. Display them on sideboards and dressers, and use jugs to hold breadsticks or celery, or a bunch of fresh flowers.

DINING-ROOM CHECKPOINTS

● Keep lighting soft and atmospheric: avoid harsh overhead lights and make the most of candlelight.

● Choose colours that are comfortable and restful to spend time with. This goes for your china too – remember that it will be the background to the colours of the food you serve.

● If your dining area is part of another room, look for folding furniture that can be stored flat when not in use.

● Use screens and curtains to partition a dual-purpose room and make the dining area feel cosy and enclosed.

● Make use of portable furniture like butler's trays to add additional storage and serving surfaces.

● Make the most of fabrics – to dress chairs and tables, and to match table linen to other furnishings.

● Use your china as part of the decoration, displayed on shelves and plate racks.

Bedrooms

There's a strong territorial sense about bedrooms. They don't need a lock on the door to convey the impression of privacy and individuality. So how do you go about shaping the identity of your own personal retreat?

We probably spend more time each day in this one room than in any other, and yet most of that time we're not even awake to notice what it looks like. So its most important task is to supply a reassuring, comfortable setting in which to sleep, and a practical place to store clothes. But the chances are that you'll also want to use it to read or relax in – and if this is the only space in your home you can really call your own, you may want to make it your own private sitting room.

COLOUR AND STYLE
The wonderful thing about bedrooms is that because they represent your own private part of the house – as opposed to the rooms that everyone uses during the day – you won't be trying to keep everyone happy, from your guests to your neighbours to your mother-in-law. So this is where you can indulge your own decorative ideas and do whatever you want to make it feel restful to you. Moreover, bedrooms are the one thing your home may have several of, so you can actually experiment with different styles in different rooms.

The other big advantage of bedrooms is that one of the strongest elements in them is fabric, so they're easy to adapt and revamp. Different bed linen, bed covers, curtains and cushions will give a completely new look, and for the ultimate cover-up you can swathe the whole thing in a different pattern or colour.

Colour is the most important element in creating mood in a bedroom, and can make it a restful or a stimulating setting according to what you want. Pinks, pale blues and greens and turquoise are conducive to relaxation and tranquillity, for instance, but if you're the sort of person who has no difficulty getting off to sleep anyway, you may be more concerned to devise a sunny yellow colour scheme that will help you wake up in the morning!

Think carefully before you add too much pattern to a bedroom. An all-over wall pattern can feel very dominant and difficult to sleep with, and plain wall colours are a much easier background to furnish. There's plenty of scope for supplying it in smaller portions with bed linen and curtain fabric, so it's better to start with these and build up the design rather than smothering it in floral wallpaper.

BEDROOM LIGHTING
Bedrooms that are just for sleeping in will need minimal lighting. A restful background glow can be provided by side lamps, and the overall effect can be controlled by dimmer switches to suit different times of day. Candlestick lamps with small shades look effective on mantelpieces and

▶ *This bedroom is so small that the best way of using the space was to position the bed in front of the window – so the window treatment has been specially designed to do double duty as curtains and a bed head. There are two layers of fabric: a light, filmy muslin which can be pulled across to add privacy in daytime too, and a heavier patterned cotton. The heading was cut as a scalloped pelmet and fixed to a wire half-hoop to make it stand out in a curve from the window, and the curtains are gathered into cord tie-backs at either side of the bed. Plain white bed linen – and a white ceiling to reflect the light from the window – instantly makes a dark basement bedroom look brighter.*

INSTANT BEDROOM STYLES

Lacy and romantic Lace is wonderful for building up layers of colour – a lace top cover on the bed will let the underlying colour show through. Try blues, greens and creams rather than pinks, to stop the effect feeling too frilly.

Neutral and understated A contemporary feel, in restful creams, whites and natural shades. Divan-style beds, or a simple frame in plain wood or metal. Plain linen curtains over white cotton blinds with rope or cord tie-backs. Plain wooden floorboards or natural floorcoverings like sisal or jute.

Simple country style Plain cream cotton or calico edged with sprigged florals or checks for bed linen and curtains. Patchwork quilts and cushions. Tapestry and samplers on the walls. Floors and furniture can be painted and stencilled to fit the scheme.

Traditional and floral An easy way to combine your favourite colours in patterned fabrics and, if you want, wallcoverings too. Lends itself to extravagant flounces of material: window pelmets, frilled bed covers and so on. If the pattern feels too rich, try mixing in plain white – a couple of crisp cotton pillows, or a lace panel at the window.

Rich and mysterious Walls in exotic colours like turquoise, deep pink or spicy cinnamon. Oriental-patterned fabrics and rugs. Add to the luxurious effect with a bed canopy or wall hanging.

bed-side tables. You'll also want reading lamps beside the bed and for work areas. Wall-mounted downlighters fixed above the bed may give a better beam, and you might consider fitting these over a dressing table or vanity unit too. Or a strip light can be fixed under a set of book shelves to illuminate a desk beneath it.

For more ideas see chapter on Lighting.

BEDROOM FLOORS

Carpet will be your first choice, for softness and warmth under bare feet as you get out of bed, and you can also use it to add more colour to your scheme. If you'd rather have one of the natural floorcoverings, check the feel of the surface first to make sure that it won't be too scratchy to the skin – jute is one of the softest. Wooden floors look good in traditional-style rooms, but you'll probably want a few soft rugs too, at least next to the bed. If you don't want plain boards, a bedroom is a good place to try out painted floors and stencilled designs, as the surface will keep its finish better than in more heavy-duty rooms.

For more ideas see chapter on Floors.

BEDROOM FURNITURE
Fitting It All In

Shortage of space in a bedroom isn't aided by the fact that the one essential item of furniture – the bed itself – is so cumbersome. Bunk beds help out in children's rooms, but where double beds are concerned even the most compact size will eat a big chunk out of a small room. In a bedroom with a high ceiling, one solution is to rig the bed up on a gallery or platform to provide space below for storage, book shelves, clothes hanging, even a desk or sewing table.

In attic rooms, or where sloping ceilings mean there's even less space, extra-careful planning will be necessary. One option is to make use of a low-ceilinged area to house the bed itself (as it won't matter if you can't stand at full height here) or designate it as 'sitting room only' – to take a desk or work table, for instance, with the sloping wall above it used as a display board.

Bed Shapes and Styles

A good, well-constructed bed is vital for your health and comfort, so don't let yourself be tempted solely by an attractive design. There's no substitute for actually trying out the bed: if you're buying a new one, don't feel inhibited about asking to test it in the shop and lying on it in different positions.

But you will also be influenced by the size and manoeuvrability of the bed, by any storage space it offers such as drawers in the base, and of course by what it looks like. A plain divan base is the neatest option, but if you've the space, a frame will contribute to the decorative style of the room, and there are plenty of designs to choose from nowadays. Wood will suit most rooms — look for light pine or oak for a modern or country-style setting, darker polished woods for a more traditional room. Cane or wicker recreates a classic colonial or plantation look. Old-fashioned brass bedsteads look magnificent if you've got the space, but the newer wrought-iron designs take up less room and suit more contemporary styles of furnishing.

Dressing the Bed

Using extra fabric to make canopies and bed hangings adds a wonderfully luxurious feel to a bedroom. You can even create your own four-poster effect by fitting a wooden frame around a plain divan base. There's no need for it to look fusty or old-fashioned — plain pine and contemporary fabric will update the effect into something quite fresh and practical.

If you don't want to go quite as far as a four-poster, you can devise your own alternative curtains and hangings. A rug or length of heavy fabric can be hung like a tapestry from a curtain pole against the bed head wall, or suspended in a canopy over the bed itelf. Lighter-weight curtains can be gathered into a coronet for a really dramatic effect, or you can drape muslin mosquito-net-style from a ceiling fitting, to swathe the whole bed in a filmy haze.

Old or unattractive headboards and foot-boards are easy to dress with new fabric covers,

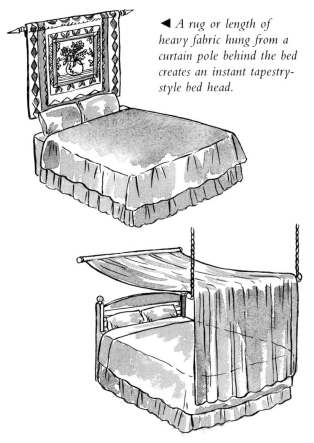

◀ A rug or length of heavy fabric hung from a curtain pole behind the bed creates an instant tapestry-style bed head.

▲ Two lengths of wood dowelling can be fixed to support a bed canopy. The pole at the head end is fixed to the wall; the one at the foot is hung on ropes or cords screwed into the ceiling, like a trapeze. Allow enough fabric to let it dip in the middle, so that its weight keeps the hanging support in place.

▼ A short length of dowelling screwed into the wall above the bed supports a length of fabric draped into curtains. Tie-backs fixed to the wall gather the fabric aside, clear of the bed itself. This effect can also be used to dress the window, to give the room a unified look.

99

▲ *Headboards and footboards are easy to cover with fabric cases. The top cover is cut from a single piece of fabric, draped over the bed frame and shaped to fit around the wooden posts. The sides are simply tied into place with fabric bows. Alternatively, a couple of extra pillows covered with pretty fabric make a hanging headboard on a curtain pole.*

either slipped over like a pillow case or attached in two panels tied with bows around the edge. And you can make your own wall-hung head-board from deep cushions or pillows, covered in fabric to match your bed covers and tied or stitched on to a curtain pole or length of dowelling fixed above the bed head.

Clothes and Storage

The key is to think about all the things you need space for and then work out storage to fit them. For instance, suits and separates don't need so much hanging space as dresses. A two-tier rail system will let you hang skirts, shirts, jackets and trousers in two rows one above the other. Or you could have a single hanging rail fronted by a

▶ *Dressing the bed imaginatively will make all the difference to a featureless room. This bed has been turned into a contemporary four-poster by adding a simple wooden frame. Fabric can be draped over the bed head to make a canopy, or hung as curtains around the sides (this is very easy to do with tie-on curtains). The general effect stays very uncluttered, and perfectly in keeping with the modern built-in cupboards. The mix of floral and plain white bed linen adds a slightly country feel.*

pretty curtain and topped by a glass or wooden surface to make an instant built-in dressing table.

Many of the bits and pieces that we keep in our bedrooms can stay out on show where they're near at hand when we want them. Peg rails and decorative hooks provide accessible storage for laundry bags, scarves, belts, ties and so on. Try running a peg rail school-cloakroom-style along one wall, topped by a narrow book or display shelf.

Make use of the space beneath the bed too. If you're buying a new bed, look for a design with storage drawers built into the base. With a bedstead that clears the floor, you can slide crates and baskets underneath to create the same effect.

QUICK-CHANGE BEDROOMS

If you live in a studio apartment without a separate bedroom, or if your spare room spends most of its time masquerading as something else – a study or office, for instance – you need to be able to turn it into a bedroom at a moment's notice. Blanket chests, window seats, peg rails and hooks will be particularly useful for storage.

The bed itself is less easy to disguise, although a single bed can be dressed quite effectively as a sofa with coverings and cushions. A dual-purpose futon or sofa bed will provide seating during the

▲ *Half-length hanging space can be fitted beneath a dressing-table top.*

day and open out into a full-size bed when needed. (If this is to be your regular sleeping place, though, make sure that you choose a sofa bed that will give enough mattress support: many are designed only for occasional use.) Even cleverer are specially designed beds that fold away completely into the wall, bedding and all, so you don't need to rearrange the room every morning when you get up. These can be hidden neatly away behind doors to look like a slim wall cupboard or wardrobe.

▼ *Make use of floor space beneath a bedstead for storing clothes and bed linen in pull-out baskets.*

▶ *Beds with drawers in the base provide useful extra storage.*

▲ *Take a tip from the clever storage ideas designed for fitted bedroom furniture. Basket drawers and two-tier hanging rails make more use of the space.*

A NEW LOOK FOR OLD CUPBOARDS

Slatted louvred doors were very popular for built-in wardrobes in the 1970s, and although these have the advantage of letting air circulate so that clothes don't get musty, they can look rather like ventilation grilles, as there's no light visible behind them. For an instant transformation, simply paint over the top to turn them into traditional Mediterranean-style shutters.

Another easy way to revamp them into something prettier is to line the panels with fabric instead. There are two ways of doing this:

1 The quickest method is to leave the slats in place and simply thread a length of fabric through the top and bottom spaces to cover them. Measure the panel width and cut the fabric a little wider so that you can turn the edges before feeding it through. For economy, you can just cover the front, and tack the fabric in place on the back of the door, but it's neater if you use a double length so that it hides the slats on the inside of the cupboard too. If you trim the fabric ends with a row of press-studs to fix them in place, the panels will be easy to remove for washing or if you want to change them for a different material.

2 The alternative is to remove the slats altogether – this gives you a greater choice of effects to create. You can fix curtain wire above and below the empty panel on the back of the door, and gather a length of fabric on to it so that it gives a pleated effect from the front. Or you can fit the empty panel with a piece of plywood covered with fabric and tacked on to the back of the door. Fronting the panel with chicken wire will add extra interest: this looks good over both gathered and plain fabrics, and you don't need to stiffen the fabric with board. The wire can be spray-painted (before you fit it!) if you want it to look less functional – white or cream, or a colour picked out from the fabric will look very effective.

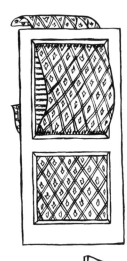

◀ *To cover the slats of a louvred cupboard door, simply loop a length of fabric through them and fasten behind with press-studs.*

▶ *The slats can be replaced completely with a fabric gathered on to curtain wires on the back of the door.*

Back   *Front*

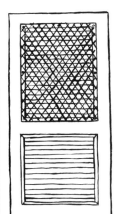

Fig. 1   *Fig. 2*   *Fig. 3*

▲ *Chicken wire stretched over fabric makes a neat finish to a cupboard door. Tack the wire in place on the reverse side of the door first (Fig. 1), then add a panel of fabric to back it (Fig. 2). Front view (finished) (Fig. 3).*

BEDROOM WINDOWS

How you dress the window(s) of your bedroom will depend partly on how much you're going to use it as a daytime room. You may want to let in as much daylight as possible, or you may prefer to preserve an enclosed, hidden-away feel. Either way, privacy will be a priority, particularly in a ground-floor apartment, so you may want to hang some sort of muslin or lace curtain which will mask the glass without obscuring the light.

The key point with window fabrics is of course that they will have to match or co-ordinate with your bed linen. You may not want more of the same, but it will have to fit in with the overall scheme. The chapters on Colour and Pattern and Windows have lots of ideas for mixing different fabrics and creating various effects – and remember that extravagant flourishes like bed coronets and canopies can be copied to dress bedroom windows too. If you're still not feeling confident enough to combine contrasting fabrics, off-the-shelf bedroom ranges help by putting together bed linen and curtains in specially co-ordinated collections, complete with tie-backs and swags or pelmets.

BEDROOM DETAILS

Pillows and cushions   These add warmth and comfort, and can be changed or rearranged when you want a different look. Mix different pillow sizes to pile on a little luxury.

Mirrors   Try them out for the best light and position: this is one room where it's a good idea to place one mirror opposite another, so that you can see your back view. Swivel-pivoted mirrors – either floorstanding or table-top – can be angled to exactly the view you want. A wash-stand or console table with a freestanding cheval mirror or a glass fixed to the wall above it creates a dressing-table effect if you haven't budget or space for the real thing.

Towel rails   Old-fashioned wooden stands with rails for two or three towels are just as good for hanging trousers flat, and for scarves, sashes, belts and beads.

Ceramics   Make use of pretty china dishes for make-up and jewellery. Jugs will hold make-up brushes, emery boards, combs and so on.

Samplers and embroideries   Frame these to hang on bedroom walls. Designs can be worked specially to commemorate the date a house was built or moved into, or with a baby's name and birthday for a nursery.

BEDROOM CHECKPOINTS

● Choose restful colours that will let you sleep easily.

● Keep lighting soft and atmospheric, using side lamps instead of overhead lights.

● Make your bed fabrics part of your colour scheme, using extra fabric and throws to soften the effect of the room and to change the look as often as you want.

● Make the most of wardrobe space by fitting two-tier hanging rails and pull-out basket drawers.

● Look for beds with drawers in the base, and improvize extra storage from boxes and baskets in different sizes.

● Look out for ways of making furniture dual-purpose: a bed-side table that doubles as a desk, a blanket box for bed linen that can be piled with cushions and turned into a window seat.

▶ *When space is very short, a bed designed as part of a run of fitted cupboards is a brilliant idea. This single bed is designed rather like a ship's bunk, with a couple of deep cupboards beneath it and extra storage above (out of sight). A simple pelmet cut from plywood trims the front of the alcove, which is lined with wood panelling and painted to match the surrounding units. It even has its own wall lights to read by. This would be ideal for a studio room.*

Bathrooms

Almost always short on space, bathrooms take a lot of planning and give little room for manoeuvre. But you can do a great deal with the right choice of colours and accessories. Try not to feel too restricted by cramped quarters and functional fittings – accept the challenge and fight back by adding pretty details like ceramics and linens to soften the clinical edge.

The first part of this chapter deals with planning a new bathroom from scratch. But if you have to make do with the last set of bathroom fittings that were installed, there are plenty of decorating and colour-scheming ideas further on to help you turn it into the room you want.

PRACTICAL THINKING
Your biggest obstacle is likely to be lack of space. A few bathrooms are large enough to feel like a room in the normal sense, with proper furniture, space to move around it – and the chance to site the bath where it gives you the best view. But many feel more like a cupboard or corridor, equipped with a few essential units fitted jigsaw-fashion in the only places they'll go.

If your new bathroom is waiting to be fitted out from scratch, you should make the most of the opportunity to use the space for the best possible layout. Draw up your floor plan on a grid as you would a kitchen plan: bathroom suppliers can give you standard measurements for different styles of fitting, and will often provide a professional planning service too.

Traditional rectangular baths come in different lengths, including short half-length sizes for where there isn't room for a full-size bath. If your bathroom is small, avoid the wider baths with rounded corners and curved side panels, and go for a narrow, square-cut shape which will be a neater fit. Corner baths are a good space-saving option for square bathrooms. In a very small flat you might even decide to do without a bath altogether and fit a shower unit instead.

Consider what storage space you need for towels, laundry and toiletries. Cupboards can be built in around the wash basin and into the bath housing itself. If you can afford the space, it's a good idea to extend a tiled or wood surface around the sides of the bath so that it makes a shelf to keep soap and shampoo within easy reach.

If you have the choice of where to put your bath, make the most of it by positioning your taps exactly where you want them too. You'll find them uncomfortable to lean against, so if you want a view across the room, it might be best to site the taps at the end of the bath that juts out into the room: not the obvious choice if you look at most bathroom designs. Or site them centrally on one side if this feels more comfortable.

▶ *Blue and white always work well in a bathroom, and here the whole effect is kept neat and trim by the unifying striped theme. The vertical stripes could have made a narrow room like this feel too tall and thin, but keeping the ceiling and floor plain white widens the space as much as possible, and the horizontal lines of the louvred window shutters balance the effect perfectly. The advantage of a tall window is of course that you can screen just the lower half while still letting plenty of light in – but the drawback is that the higher part can be difficult to reach. In this bathroom the problem has been solved by designing the top shutter section to lift upwards on a pole mechanism, so it can be manoeuvred easily from floor level.*

▲ *Vertical radiators are very useful where there isn't much free wall space lower down, and a ladder radiator acts as a towel rail too.*

COLOUR AND STYLE

In a relatively small space like this, where there isn't much room for actual furniture, colour – even if it's only black and white – is the key decorative element. It can make the room look larger or warmer and soften the effect of functional fittings. If you haven't the budget or the confidence to redecorate yet, simply introducing coloured towels and china will make all the difference.

Colours for Fittings

Bathroom fittings come in a host of colours nowadays, from pretty pastels right through to deep navy and burgundy. The range available is a great advantage if you're doing the choosing, but not so much help if you are having to find paint colours, tiles or towels to match someone else's selection! So as well as advising which colours to choose for a new suite, this section suggests how to colour scheme around an existing one, including some of the more difficult shades.

You'll make life a lot easier for yourself if you fit a white bathroom suite. As well as giving you the greatest freedom in choosing decorating colours to start with, it will also be much less

trouble to work around when you next decide you want to redecorate.

The next best option are the very pale pastels: pinks, creams, beiges and lavender-greys. In terms of matching other colours, you can treat them more or less as pure white, and if you find white too clinical, these will give a slightly warmer feel to the room.

Bathroom suites in bolder colours have two big disadvantages. First, they are are far harder to match. And second, you must be prepared to clean and rinse them scrupulously – the darker the colour, the more clearly soapy tide marks show up! If you want a strong colour, blues and greens are the easiest to work with, partly because they are natural 'water' colours that feel at home in a bathroom, and partly because they are easy shades to colour scheme with. A blue bath can be offset by green, yellow or bright scarlet towels and accessories, while a green bath will work with pinks (for a flowery, country-cottage feel) or bright blues and yellows to create a splashy, Caribbean look.

The really difficult colours to match are the murky shades like avocado, caramel and burgundy. These have a dense, heavy quality that's just not in keeping with a bathroom. In fact if you're stuck with one of these, it's best not to try to match it at all, but to lighten the effect with plenty of white and cream for towels and wall colours. White will cool down the hot, sticky look of an orange or caramel suite. Burgundy is better paired with cream, as the stark contrast of white will make it look like a battlefield. And either white or cream – or even a soft yellow – will do a lot to improve an avocado or khaki bath.

Decorating Hints

Bathroom walls can be painted, papered, panelled or tiled, or a mixture of any of these. Paper will need to be from a waterproof range, and paint should be a washable finish such as eggshell or a specialist bathroom paint.

Tiled splashback areas around bath and wash basin are a good idea, but if you decide to tile the walls completely, choose large tiles to add a greater sense of space: a wall of small tiles will look too dense and visually confusing in a small room. A solid run of obviously patterned tiles should be avoided for the same reason – it's better to use mostly plain tiles and add a few patterned ones as an occasional feature.

Because small rooms have a large proportion of wall space in comparison with the room area, they look better if this is broken up by creating a border line half-way up. Wood panelling has taken over in popularity from tiles for this – and is particularly good if you have uneven wall surfaces you want to hide. The panelling can be topped with a narrow shelf to provide extra storage for toiletries, and extending it to box in the bath as well gives the whole room a neat, streamlined look. Make sure that the wood is well sealed so that it won't be affected by damp and steam, and paint it in a washable finish.

BATHROOM LIGHTING

Many bathrooms in flats and apartments have no exterior wall and therefore no windows at all. And what windows there are are likely to be screened for privacy. So your first priority will be to provide a good source of overall light. Remember that bathroom light fittings will have

▲ *Wooden wall panelling continued around the sides of the bath gives a neat, streamlined effect.*

INSTANT BATHROOM STYLES

Beach house Light blues, aquas and plenty of white. White-painted or bleached wood panelling. Shell soap dishes and other seaside-style accessories. Plain white curtains or pale stripes or simple checks. Wooden duckboards on the floor.

Victorian The sort of room that should really have an old roll-top bath – but you can still create the look with accessories. Delft-style blue and white tiles. Plain white towels. Patterned china. Ceramic loo handles. Old washstands (if there's room) with an old-fashioned water pitcher and basin. Big old-fashioned cross-head taps.

Caribbean Blues and greens with splashes of red and yellow. Lots of plants. Mirrors with bright-painted wooden frames. Flying fish and parrot motifs on fabrics and accessories.

Spruce and nautical Dark polished wood panelling and loo seat. Brass fittings. Navy and white towels and tiles. Traditional striped wallpaper.

Pretty and cottagey Light woods – pine loo set and pine-framed mirrors. Pink and green towels and floral fabrics. Pretty china and baskets to hold make-up and toiletries.

Smart and jazzy Black-and-white tiled floors and walls in geometric patterns. Chrome fittings. High-tech ladder radiators. Towels and accessories in bold primary colours.

to be enclosed for safety, and controlled by a pull cord or a switch outside the room so that there's no risk of touching live switches with wet hands.

The most practical option, especially if the ceiling is low, is ceiling-recessed downlighters, as they won't get in the way of towels when you're drying yourself. If rewiring the ceiling isn't possible, enclosed glass shades can be fitted on either ceiling or wall-mounted lights. You'll want task lighting to illuminate mirrors and possibly vanity units or dressing tables. Some mirror units have an integral light. If you've a large mirror, you can create a very effective film-star dressing-room look by fitting a row of plain low-wattage pearl bulbs fixed into battens down either side, or across the top.

◀ *Plain bulbs fitted around a mirror turn a bathroom into a film-star dressing room.*

BATHROOM FLOORS

Bathroom floors need to be comfortable, water-proof and non-slip.

Ceramic tiles may be within your budget for a small room, and they can also increase the sense of floor space if you choose a light colour. Marble-effect ceramics look very effective if you want a feeling of real luxury! Ceramics are easy to slip on, though – you'll want to be especially careful if the bathroom will be used by children. Vinyl is cheaper and warmer, and provides the same variety of colour.

Cork tiles or wood will be warm underfoot and give a warmer visual effect too. If you want a wood floor to look more spacious, you can paint floorboards in a light colour for a traditional beach-house look – pale woodstrip flooring will give the same effect. Cork and wood both need sealing to make them waterproof.

Waterproof carpet is a godsend for anyone who can't bear to step out of a warm bath on to a cold floor. Waffle-backed against the damp, it also comes in a versatile range of colours.

To take the cold edge off hard floors and provide a non-slippery surface for wet feet, bath mats are a useful addition.

For more ideas see chapter on Floors.

BATHROOM WINDOWS

The main problem facing a bathroom window is to let in daylight without reducing privacy, so you might want to make use of some of the ideas suggested for windows in Chapter 10, to screen the window with a light cotton blind or half-length panel.

Too much elaborate fabric can look over-dressed and unwieldy in a bathroom, but you can still add pattern and colour by fitting a plain roller blind. Or fit a single curtain which can be pulled to one side in a tie-back. Seaside stripes look effective tied back with rope. Plain white can be trimmed with a fabric that matches the shade of a coloured suite.

Wooden shutters are a neat solution for a small bathroom. And if you've got the time and the discipline to care for them, a collection of plants can provide an alternative curtain, and will filter a restful green light into the room.

◀ *Red isn't an obvious colour choice for a bathroom, but the rich terracotta and cream here really warm up what was rather a cold, sunless area. Building the bath and basin into panelled surrounds makes the whole effect feel less clinical and more like a room, as well as providing a useful shelf around the bath to hold toiletries. The window is fitted with a simple roller blind to maximize light, but the room doesn't go without curtains altogether – gathered fabric has been used to line the cupboard doors, adding colour and appropriate seaside-style motifs, and again maintaining a comfortable, 'furnished' effect. Keeping toiletries and accessories on display on shelves and in open containers adds pattern to a plain background.*

BATHROOM DETAILS

Linens   Towels, flannels, bath robes, rugs and shower curtains are an instant way of adding colour. Make up leftover curtain or blind fabric into drawstring bags that will hang on a peg rail or on the back of the door – a large one for laundry or clean socks, smaller ones as make-up and wash bags.

Towel rails   Can be wall-hung or floor-standing. Heated rails plumbed into your heating system are particularly useful so that towels dry quickly after use – some of the most stylish (and expensive!) wall radiators provide a series of bars in a vertical ladder effect. Old-fashioned wooden towel stands give a more traditional 'furnished' effect if you've got the floor space.

Shelves and racks   Wall cabinets won't hold more than the essentials, and shampoo, cleansers, spare soap and so on are best kept out on open shelves where you can reach them from the bath.

Hooks and pegs   Extra hanging space for towels as well as flannels, wash bags, bath brushes and so on. Bathroom linens will all dry faster if they can hang rather than sitting around on a damp surface. A peg rail topped by a narrow ledge will help keep a small room free of clutter and provide shelf storage for toiletries.

▲ *A narrow shelf at dado height will provide a decorative border and keep essential toiletries near at hand. Peg-rail hanging storage is especially useful for bathrooms as it lets damp items dry more quickly.*

BATHROOM CHECKPOINTS

● You can't get away from the basic bathroom appliances, so add colour and accessories for decorative effect.

● If you have the chance to plan from scratch, make the most of the different sizes and styles for baths, basins and fittings that give you the maximum space.

● Consult a plumbing professional before deciding on any changes that will involve moving pipework and waste positions.

● Make sure that there's enough room to manoeuvre around each appliance.

● Don't box in pipework so securely that you can't get to it in an emergency.

Containers   Make use of pretty mugs, jugs, vases and dishes to hold toothbrushes, toothpaste, make-up brushes and so on. Hide bathroom cleaners and cloths neatly out of sight in a painted box or wicker hamper.

Mirrors   Can be incorporated into cabinet doors or fixed as a separate fitting. In a small room, any design that increases access and flexibility is an advantage, so look for swivel-head mirrors that can be adjusted for the best light and extending shaving glasses that pull out from the wall concertina-style.

▶ *The mixture of painted woodwork with white walls, fittings and linens gives a very practical feel to this restful sea-green bathroom. It's a slightly old-fashioned look, but without being cluttered – the simple fabric pelmet is a particularly clever idea for a small window like this. The decorative towel rail and carved wall cabinet show how pretty accessories can stop a bathroom from feeling functional.*

Last Details

When you've spent all that time and effort – and most of your furnishing budget – on decorating your home, adding the details becomes great fun. This is what puts your personal stamp on the place. The best accessories give instant impact for very little cost, and choosing them or making your own is one of the nicest parts of decorating.

The accessories you add will make all the difference to a finished room. They can pull a colour scheme together, add interest to a bare wall, smarten up a shabby piece of furniture and make a feature of an unnoticed corner. This chapter supplements the ideas suggested for individual rooms throughout the book. It includes purely decorative details just for fun, and practical items that benefit from looking good too. Use them as a starting point: once you've got the hang of experimenting with paint, paper and fabric, and learning how to arrange things for effect, you'll find inspiration in a hundred different places.

The secret is to be prepared to adapt and update. Never throw away something you're fond of just because it doesn't match or is looking a little the worse for wear. Remember that chairs can be painted or re-covered. Curtains can be trimmed with contrasting pelmets or tie-backs. Shabby old picture and mirror frames can be painted to match a colour scheme, or just to smarten them up.

Build up a stock of fabric remnants and trimmings so that you can add matching detail to assorted soft furnishings. A set of co-ordinating cushions will unify a medley of odd armchairs. Even cushions in different fabrics can be piped or buttoned in a single accent colour to make them into a set.

Think laterally about how to put decorative items to effective use. There are so many ornamental details available in the shops these days – trimmings, tie-backs, curtain-pole finials, decorative hooks and handles – that it's a shame not to make the most of them. Collect individual things you like and look for a use for them later.

Before you start, invest in a few essential tools that will make the job of revamping and accessorizing much easier. A staple gun is invaluable – quicker than sewing or pasting for any re-covering task using fabric or paper. And an eyelet punch will make instant ready-bound holes in a fabric edge, ready for hooking or tying into place. Eyelet kits can be bought from the haberdashery sections of department stores. (Metal eyelets like these are used as fixings on boat sails, so you can usually buy slightly more heavyweight punch kits from ships' chandlers and sailing suppliers.)

DISPLAYING A COLLECTION

The key to making a good display on a shelf or table top is to find a unifying factor – a colour, shape or style that makes the items look like a

▶ *All sorts of clever details have been used to furnish this small dining area. A narrow wallpaper border has been used to make fake panels on the wall, giving the picture an instant frame and also matching the table cloth fabric. Tie-on covers in the same colours effectively disguise the dark wood of the chairs. Candle sconces provide wall decoration as well, and an old enamel colander makes an impromptu fruit bowl.*

115

collection, not just a lot of unrelated bits and pieces. It doesn't matter how simple they are: they make an impact just by being massed together.

China and glass are traditional display items, so they're an easy place to start. Try grouping together a collection of china all one colour, or chequered mugs in different colours, or jugs of different sizes, or oddments of traditional floral china. Don't worry if they're not in perfect condition – the beauty of a massed display is that the odd chip or crack won't show! Coloured glass bottles or vases look particularly effective on a window sill so that the light shines through them.

Bear in mind that there's no limit to the sort of thing you can turn into a display, so don't confine yourself to conventional ornaments. Dig out your childhood toy cars and line them up along a shelf. And a bowl of glass marbles or smooth beach pebbles or pretty shells is really all you need to put the finishing touch to a sitting-room table or bedroom chest.

Finally don't forget flowers. The same rules work for flowers as for other display items, so you're better off massing together lots of yellow tulips or white daisies in one vase than trying to create a formal masterpiece. The best flower arrangements are always the simplest. But remember that some of the most effective details work because they combine unusual elements not normally seen together, so if you haven't enough vases, make use of teapots, milk jugs and other serviceable containers that emphasize the beauty of the flowers by contrast.

◄ *Colours, textures and clever grouping work perfectly here to accessorize a small room. Putting simple objects together always makes more of an impression than displaying them individually, and blue-and-white china is one of the foolproof combinations. It doesn't seem to matter how many different patterns and shades you mix, they never fail to look good. To match the wood furniture, the shelf also holds a basket of dried flowers and a simple stencilled picture, but painting the shelf blue co-ordinates the whole thing.*

◄ *The simplest flower arrangements look the best, so go for colour and quantity, and mass a group of a single flower type together.*

STENCILLING AND DÉCOUPAGE

Decorative patterns created with stencilling and old-fashioned découpage techniques will dress up anything from walls to furniture to trinket boxes.

Cutting a Stencil

Shop-bought stencils are made of waxed or oiled card, or acetate. Because the patterns are cut out of them by machine, they can afford to be very intricate, giving a delicate, detailed effect on the wall or furniture surface.

If you're making your own stencils, it's best to start with a simpler design until you've got the hang of creating a pattern that will hold together in one piece. The secret for a beginner is to keep fairly sturdy 'bridges' (the pieces of card that link the motifs of your pattern). Try a basic flower head or geometric shape as an experiment.

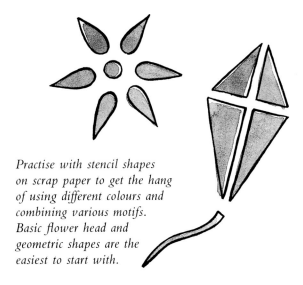

Practise with stencil shapes on scrap paper to get the hang of using different colours and combining various motifs. Basic flower head and geometric shapes are the easiest to start with.

117

▲ *The outline of a cup can be repeated to make a fake row hanging from a kitchen or dining-room shelf. If you're feeling a little more confident, you can cut out a bolder design to give it more substance.*

Draw the shape on to card with a pencil (oiled stencil-weight card can be bought from craft shops). Tape the card on to a cutting board and carefully cut out the pattern with a craft knife. Remember to keep the bridges intact: it's the shape that's left that will create your pattern, not the pieces you remove. (If you do make a mistake, you can repair the card by sticking masking tape over the area on both sides and then recutting the shape.)

Applying the Pattern

The pattern can now be transferred quite easily on to walls and woodwork – and even fabric. (Tiles and non-porous surfaces are more difficult, so don't try these until you're more practised.)

Stencil paints and crayons are available from craft shops, or you can use emulsion paint. (You'll need special fabric paint to stencil on to fabric.)

Practise on paper first, and plan which colours you want to use for different elements of the pattern. Tape the stencil securely in place with masking tape. The important thing is to keep your brush dry and apply the colour very gradually: you don't want it to seep under the card and blur your shape. Use small, circular movements and work the colour carefully into the edges of the pattern.

Once you've mastered the technique you can try more complicated patterns with more delicate bridges. Use the cup stencil shown here as a repeat design to make a whole row of 'cups' beneath a shelf unit (see the illustration on page 94). Alternatively copy a favourite cup of your own.

Decorating with Découpage

Découpage is great fun and costs nothing at all to do. It's a little like making up a scrapbook, but instead of pasting the cutout patterns into a book, you stick them on to furniture and accessories. Trinket boxes, picture and mirror frames, cupboard and door fronts, and the slats of chair backs can all be given extra decoration with this technique. And the motifs you use can be taken from all sorts of sources: giftwrap, wallpaper scraps and pictures from magazines are some of the easiest. Flower heads, stars, shells and fruit make good centrepieces – or angels and cherubs

▲ *Chair back and mirror frame with découpage decoration.*

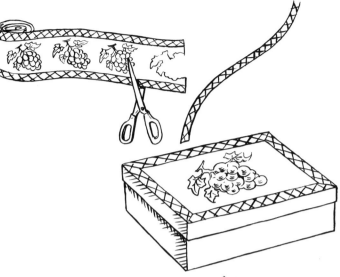

▲ *Wallpaper borders and pictures from magazines can be cut up to create stick-on découpage patterns on furniture and accessories. Anything from trinket boxes and frames to larger pieces of furniture can be decorated like this.*

if you want to be a bit more whimsical! Cutout garlands and ribbons are perfect for edging and outlining.

You'll find it easiest to work with a water-soluble glue diluted slightly so that it's not too heavy for the paper cutouts. To protect patterns on furniture and small items that may be handled a lot, it's best to add a coat of clear varnish over the top. Shellac (available from art shops) is the easiest to use as it dries quickly. You can also make the effect look like a genuine antique by giving it a crackle-glazed surface – this is good for small wooden trinket boxes and picture or mirror frames. Specially formulated crackle-glaze is available from art shops, complete with instructions. You simply paint it on in two layers, and the surface cracks as it dries.

Craft shops have cottoned on to the popularity of decorating with paper patterns and many now sell sheets of motifs ready for you to cut out. Remember that black-and-white designs often look just as good as colours, so you can always photocopy a motif and re-use it as often as you want.

▲ *You can photocopy the motifs shown here to cut out and use for découpage decorations.*

119

PAPER PANELLING

Don't reserve pretty lining paper for the dark recesses of drawer bases. Use wallpaper or heavyweight giftwrap to line the backs of open shelves and glass cabinets. You can even add pattern to a door by cutting paper to fit the panels. If it's a flat door, make your own panels from wood moulding and stick them on so that they cover the raw paper edges.

Door panels and shelf backs can be lined with wallpaper or giftwrap to add patterned detail to a plain wall.

PICTURE SHOW

You don't need to collect old masters to make an effective display of pictures on a wall. Favourite photos and pages from magazines will provide an instant gallery if you put them in matching frames. (And odd frames can easily be painted to turn them into a set.) Quantity is more important than quality here: the trick is to group them so that they create a massed effect that disguises any individual imperfections! A collection of pictures all the same size can be grouped symmetrically – four of them in a square, three large posters in a row, or a whole line of them up your staircase.

If they're all odd sizes, you need to experiment a little. Lay them out on the floor and try fitting them together in different positions like a jigsaw. The best shape to aim for is an inverted triangle

▲ *Pictures make more impact when displayed as a group. Aim for a basic triangular pattern on a plain wall, or hang them in a row to make a gallery on a staircase.*

of some sort, so that the largest pictures and the emphasis of the group is at the top – this keeps the whole display as an eye-level focal point.

There's no need to stop at pictures either. Almost anything can be framed, from a collection of theatre programmes to an assortment of holiday souvenirs. Framed certificates and job rejections will provide entertaining reading on a loo wall!

Instant Framework
You can also create your own decorative picture borders with paper or paintwork. This is a good way of highlighting a small, symmetrical group of pictures. Try putting a border around the group so that it frames them completely – a narrow wallpaper border is ideal. If you're feeling more adventurous, you can design a decorative heading giving a *trompe l'oeil* effect of cords, bows and tassels. Look for stencil patterns with the motifs you want – or you may find a wallpaper border with a design you can cut out and stick on (follow the instructions for découpage on pages 118–19).

▲ Trompe l'oeil *decoration can make your pictures look as though they are traditionally hung with bows and tassels. Use a ready-made fabric or plaster bow, or add a painted or stencilled design of your own.*

Even easier, pictures from books or magazines can be pasted straight on to the wall and framed with a home-made border. You'll need a good, flat wall surface for this (don't try doing it on woodchip wallpaper), but it looks very effective and costs nothing at all. Stick to a theme: black-and-white prints of maps or botanical drawings work particularly well, and you can even use a photocopy if you don't want to cut up a book.

▼ *A collection of traditional accessories that show how easy it is to add colour and instant style to a room. Cushions and bolsters can be made in all sorts of shapes and fabrics – for maximum impact mix different patterns in toning colours. Tie-backs provide practical trimming for curtains. And old-fashioned suitcases and hatboxes give you instant storage space for small items.*

▲ *Plain black-and-white prints of maps and architectural drawings can be pasted straight on to a flat wall surface and framed with a simple wallpaper border.*

BUTTONS, BOWS AND TASSELS

Buttons are making a comeback, having been shamed into years of oblivion by the invisible charms of the zip fastener. Neat and pretty, they can smarten up cushions, pillow cases, bed covers, curtains, upholstery – anything that might otherwise be zipped up or snapped shut with a discreet press-stud. But they don't actually

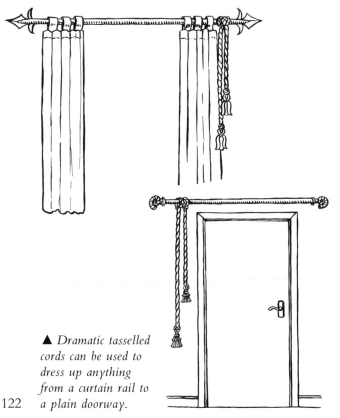

▲ *Dramatic tasselled cords can be used to dress up anything from a curtain rail to a plain doorway.*

have to funtion to look good, so if you're daunted by the thought of edging all those buttonholes, just use them as decorative trimming and keep the zip to do the work!

Bows make quick-tie fastenings. Stitch small strips of fabric into the edging of chair covers so that you can tie the corners with a neat row of bows – and undo them in a few seconds to remove for cleaning. Trim curtains with bows to tie them on to the curtain pole, and you won't need to add heading tape and fiddly hooks.

Tasselled cords add a sense of drama and opulence wherever you hang them. They look wonderful hung from a curtain pole or the side of a bookcase, or positioned to frame a picture, mirror or bed head. You can even dress up a plain doorway by fixing a pole over the lintel, with a luxurious tassel hanging at one side. And you can use them to replace the nylon cords of light and heating switches.

CUSHIONS

Plump, pretty cushions add comfort, warmth and accent colour. Match them to your curtains or upholstery, or throw in a completely new fabric to liven up the scheme – a checked cushion on a floral-patterned sofa, or an old-fashioned tapestry print against a plain chair. Use lots of them together so that they look really luxurious: a pile of different colours and patterns gives a good sense of comfortable informality.

One of the easiest cushions to make is a traditional sausage-shaped bolster design. The cover can be stitched as a single cylinder. Thread a drawstring through the hem at either end so that it can be pulled tight and finished with a tassel or fabric-covered button in the centre.

Square cushions can be revamped with a loose cover over the top simply made from two squares tied together around the edges. This is a quick way to update an old cushion that doesn't match the scheme, but you can use it to add interest to new cushions too. Look for budget cushions in plain colours and pick a patterned fabric to tie over the top so that the underneath colour shows around the sides. For an extra-

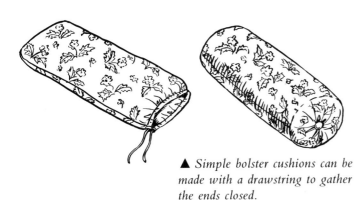

▲ *Simple bolster cushions can be made with a drawstring to gather the ends closed.*

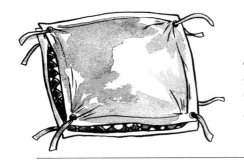

◀ *Tie-on cushion covers add contrasting colour to the pad beneath.*

Baskets are always good value – anything from a wicker picnic hamper to a deep log basket. Old-fashioned bicycle baskets are particularly useful because they have one flat side that will stand neatly against a wall. Remember that hampers and laundry baskets are especially useful for children's rooms because the lids are light enough not to hurt little fingers if they fall shut.

Shoe and boot boxes can be covered with wallpaper, fabric or giftwrap to store letters, cassettes, bills and other paperwork, or cleaning and shoe polishing equipment. (Boot boxes are an ideal size for storing letters flat.) They can be colour-coded for practicality.

For a traditional effect, old leather suitases and big circular hatboxes look very smart and can be stacked on top of one another in a corner of a bedroom. These are great for holding small items like socks, scarves and underwear. Try stacking leather cases stagecoach-style in descending order of size on a low chest or table.

quick method, you don't need to stitch the ties on to the cover – just punch three or four eyelet holes along each side and thread the ties through.

MIRRORS

As well as their obvious practical purpose, mirrors add variety to walls and reflect light. Choose them for their frames, as you would a picture, and position them where they catch a favourite view. You can group them like pictures too. The only general rule with mirrors is not to site them directly opposite one another, which results in an ever-decreasing image of one mirror reflected in the other.

STORAGE AND HIDEAWAYS

However much storage you allow for, there will always be bits and pieces that need to be found a quick and easy-to-reach home, from stationery and sewing things to children's toys. Make a virtue of necessity and keep an eye out for good-looking containers that you're happy to have on show.

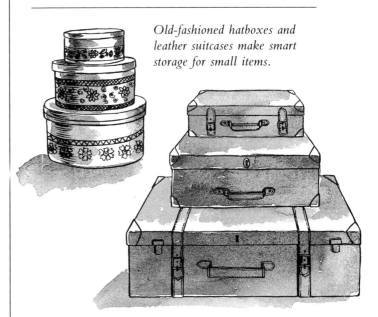

Old-fashioned hatboxes and leather suitcases make smart storage for small items.

BOOKENDS

Don't leave books lying around to get damaged just because you've run out of shelf space. Prop them between bookends to make a display on a mantelpiece or window sill. All sorts of objects can be pressed into service as long as they're

123

heavy enough to keep the books in place. Try improvizing with pot plants, architectural stone-work, or a couple of square-edged glass vases filled with marbles to weight them.

SHELF TRIMS

A set of functional shelves can be dressed up by adding a trimming of lace or ribbon along the front of each ledge. It's easy to change the decoration to match any new furnishings. For a more permanent effect, cut a simple wooden pelmet to fit the top of the unit and paint the whole thing so that it looks like a designer piece.

NAME PLATES

Bedroom doors, kitchen drawers and storage boxes all benefit from being clearly labelled. Fit them with old-fashioned brass card holders from ironmongers or hardware stores. Decorative cards can be slotted inside to remind you what you've put where, and are easy to change when you decide to have a clear-out.

NEW KNOBS AND HANDLES

Doors and furniture can be instantly improved by a little attention to detail. Replacing func-tional aluminium door handles with china, glass or antique-effect black metal knobs makes a world of difference. Wooden knobs for cup-boards and drawers can be painted to match your furnishings or wall colour.

MAKING A LATTICE PINBOARD

Use up leftover curtain fabric or wallpaper by covering a panel of plywood to make a notice-board for reminders and invitations.

Cut the fabric or paper a few centimetres larger than the plywood. Fold the edges around the board, turning the corners under as though wrapping a parcel, then staple in place all the way around. Criss-cross with lengths of ribbon or string in a trellis effect, stapling the ends of the ribbon to the back of the board and adding an extra length to make a hanging loop. You can neaten the back by covering the raw edges with another panel of paper or fabric.

▲ *Lace and ribbon can be used to trim shelf edges, and a simple wood pelmet will provide a decorative heading for a plain unit.*

▲ *Brass card holders make useful name plates for drawers and bedroom doors.*

◀ *Notice-boards for postcards and reminders are easy to make with ribbon bound trellis-style around a board covered with pretty fabric or paper.*

Glossary of Terms and Tools

Many of the terms here are described in more detail in individual chapters, but this glossary provides a quick-reference guide and explains some of the other techniques you're likely to come across when you're shopping or researching new ideas.

Advancing colours   Paint colours that make a wall or surface appear to be closer than it is – usually dark colours and shades from the warmer end of the colour spectrum, such as reds and oranges. *See also* Receding colours.

Anaglypta   Embossed wallpaper – strictly speaking a trade name, but often used more generally to describe any relief-pattern paper.

Architrave   Wood or plaster surround of a door or window.

Beading   Narrow strip of decorative wood used for trimming and edging. (Also called moulding.)

Butcher's block   Very thick chopping block, usually beechwood, fitted on a stand. Sometimes designed as a trolley to make it more manoeuvrable.

Butler's sink   Deep rectangular porcelain sink originally designed for heavyduty washing-up in sculleries and servants' kitchens.

Butler's tray   High-sided tray with sides that fold flat to form a table top which fits on to a folding stand.

Calico   Plain white or cream cotton cloth, often left unbleached. Quite stiff – good for simple curtains and instant upholstery.

Carver   Upright dining chair with wooden arms, usually designed as the 'head' chair of a set.

Casement window   Window that is hinged to open like a door.

Chaise-longue   Couch with a low back support and an arm at one end.

Chipboard   Board made of compressed wood chips. Quite heavy, but not very attractive: useful for items such as display tables that you're going to cover with a fabric cloth.

Colourwashing   Very thin, almost transparent layers of emulsion glaze giving an effect of translucent colour.

Console table   Narrow or semi-circular table designed to be stood against a wall or fixed to it with brackets.

Crackle-glazing   Finish for paints and varnishes that gives a broken surface, to make the surface look older or add variation to a solid colour.

Dado rail   Wood or plaster rail running along a wall at the height of a chair back. (Sometimes called a chair rail.)

Day bed   Wooden-framed couch designed like a bed with a support at both ends so that it stands flat against a wall.

Découpage   Cutout paper patterns used as pasted-on decoration for furniture and accessories. (Originated in the eighteenth century.)

Dhurrie   Flat Indian cotton rug, usually woven in a geometric design.

Director's chair   Upright wooden-framed folding chair with a canvas cover – the name originates from its use on film sets.

Distressing   Deliberate ageing and weathering techniques to give character to woodwork, paintwork and metal.

Divan   Bed base with no headboard or footboard.

Dowelling   Round wooden rod designed to be cut into short lengths used as fixing pins.

Dragging   A paint effect producing fine stripes in the surface, created by literally dragging a dry brush or stiff comb downwards through the glaze.

Eggshell   Oil-based paint with a low-sheen satin finish.

Finial   Ornamental endpiece: for example, for a curtain pole.

Futon   Thin mattress designed to fold up as a cushion when not being used as a bed. Sometimes comes with a low wooden frame base.

Gate-leg   Table with legs that swing sideways like a gate to allow the top to fold down.

Glaze   Thin coats of transparent or semi-transparent paint which can be layered or used to provide a top surface for a paint effect. *See also* Colourwashing.

Hold-back   Knob or bracket designed to hold curtains aside.

Key   Rough surface created (for instance, with sandpaper) to improve adhesion of paint or plaster.

Kilim   Traditional flat-woven rug of Middle Eastern design.

Louvres   Slats fitted in a door, window or shutter to allow ventilation.

Marbling   Streaked paintwork creating a veined effect in different colours, like genuine marble.

MDF   Medium-density fibreboard: reconstituted wood available in various thicknesses, very tough and warp-resistant, with a smooth surface. Good for making shaped trims such as pelmets.

Melamine   Resilient plastic used to make units and lightweight furniture with a washable surface.

Mitring   A neat corner formed by joining two pieces of wood or fabric to make a 90-degree angle.

Moulding   Ornamental strip of wood or plaster used to trim walls, ceilings and doors.

Muslin   Plain, fine, gauzy cotton, good for using as an alternative to net curtains.

Pelmet   Deep border – rigid or fabric – designed as a trimming: for example, to hide a curtain track.

Plinth   Supporting base: for instance, of kitchen units.

Plywood   Thin but strong board made from layers glued together with the direction of the grain alternating.

Quadrant   Quarter-circle shape often used as a narrow trim in materials such as ceramic tiles and wooden moulding.

Rag-rolling   Using a rag twisted into a sausage shape so that it can be rolled over a wet painted surface for a random pattern.

Ragging off/ragging on   Paint effects using a scrunched-up cotton or leather rag to create a textural pattern on a paint surface. Ragging off means dabbing the paint off in patches. Ragging on involves dipping the rag into paint or glaze and then using it to apply the pattern.

Receding colours   Colours that make a wall or surface appear to be further away than it actually is – usually pale colours, especially from the 'cooler' end of the spectrum, such as blues, greys and blue-greens.

Sconce   Wall bracket holding a candle or light fitting.

Spattering   Spraying droplets of diluted emulsion on to a painted surface by flicking the bristles of the brush. Creates a speckled granite-style finish, more modern-looking than most paint effects.

Sponging   Printing a sponged pattern on to a painted surface.

Stencilling   Patterns created by masking areas of a surface and applying colour to the exposed parts.

Ticking   Strong, close-woven twill fabric, usually worked in narrow stripes on a white background. Traditionally used to make pillows and mattresses and very versatile for upholstery and curtains.

Tie-back   Cord, rope or length of fabric used to gather curtains at the side of a window.

Toile de jouy   Fabric with a detailed pattern of traditional scenes worked in a single colour on a white or cream background.

Tongue and groove   Wood boarding that slots together to form ridged panelling.

Trompe l'oeil   Literally an effect that 'deceives the eye' – usually a painted design that looks three-dimensional.

Verdigris   Green coating that forms on copper and bronze when exposed to the atmosphere. Often faked to make modern metals look antique.

Index